THE *Soul* FREQUENCY

The author of this book does not dispense medical advice or prescribe the use of any technique as a form of treatment for physical, emotional, or medical problems without the advice of a physician, either directly or indirectly. The intent of the author is only to offer information of a general nature to help you in your quest for greater well-being. In the event you use any of the information in this book for yourself, the author assumes no responsibility for your actions.

www.TheSoulFrequency.com

Cover and interior design by Annette Wood.
www.AnnetteWoodGraphics.com

Ordering Information:
Special discounts are available on quantity purchases by corporations, associations, and others.
Please email requests to: info@thesoulfrequency.com

Printed in the United States of America

First Printing, 2018

ISBN 978-1-7325055-2-0

THE *Soul* FREQUENCY

YOUR HEALTHY,
AWAKENED AND
AUTHENTIC LIFE

SHANNA LEE

Dedication

To those with a deep desire for the truth,
those who are

seeking...

growing...

and

questioning...

Welcome home to the awakened life
that has been waiting for you.

You have a renegade heart
A true rule breaker in the most loving sense
Never bound by expectation
Living free of pretense

With the purest focused intention
You're a catalyst for forward motion
Expanding possibility, overflowing
Enough to fill an ocean

Be still in the movement
As the chorus of life sings
Through the trees, the whispers of truth
Full of excitement for the clarity it brings

Out of the darkness with gratitude
A memory of a shadow cast
The grand initiation is now
Your glory expands fast

Step over the threshold in faith
Breathe in every moment
As your heart expands and life evolves
You reach the sweetest fulfillment

Cross over the flames of fear with courage
Accessing joy and blissful youth
Arriving at your depths aware and awake
The embodiment of LOVE + TRUTH

Contents

Preface

There are levels and layers to health and healing, to consciousness and to what we understand in our current reality. We are moving from the era of information—wherein we have relied fully on linear thinking and what our five senses tell us—and into the era of intuition, where we are becoming what seem to be superhuman versions of ourselves. This book carries the energetic frequency of healing. While your brain will be amused and engaged in the processing of powerful stories, concepts, and information; your consciousness will be waking up and downloading healing, high-frequency energy that your body will assimilate and integrate. This transmission is of a benevolent, loving, and kind energy that will help you have a more joyous, healthy, and harmonious life.

This book is for those who want to heal at the deepest levels. This is not a book that presents the science of the human body, recommends a specific diet, or provides specific protocols for treating ailments. This book is communicating at a multifaceted and multidimensional level. It is not necessary for you to understand all levels of healing in order to receive all of the benefits this book has to offer. This work is for those who want to take in this powerful energy as the basis for action without going into all the processes that led to these conclusions. It is expected that the reader will take these conclusions in faith and trust the process that will begin to unfold from within. By taking inspired action you will experience the truth and wisdom within this book first hand and see evidence of it in your life.

This book will guide you through a transformational process that could last a few weeks or a few years. People are unique—no single journey is better than another's. You may find that you devour one section in a few days and take weeks to finish another. You may read the whole book only to refer back to it and realize you missed so much on the first pass. There are seeds of wisdom that will sink in based on your current perspective and ones that will land fully sometime in the future. So, go at your own pace, listen within, and see what starts to appear in your life as you receive the intention of this book in whatever timeframe your soul wants to assimilate it.

The frequency on this planet is rapidly rising, our human bodies are evolving to integrate with these new frequencies; and as a result, we are vibrating faster and able to access new forms of information and assimilate them. The world as we know it is literally speeding up. We are starting to pick up the subtle nuances of the energy around us and we intuit our lives more accurately. We are literally learning to upgrade to new versions of ourselves. A "2.0" version of you, of me, of everyone on the planet is being born and is able to perceive life in new ways.

Preface

As we upgrade our energy system and our perception of life, we must offload the blocks, limitations, and fears that have kept our bodies dense and in resonance with unhealthy states of being. This process can feel unsettling until you understand exactly what and why it is happening—and then it becomes empowering. While it might seem that the world is becoming unhealthier, more chaotic, or emotionally desensitized, this is actually serving a purpose. It is waking us up.

Chaos is often the predecessor of change. In the process of becoming more sensitive in our bodies, we naturally begin to purge anything toxic within us emotionally, mentally, and physically, which can often be a somewhat uncomfortable experience. We may also manifest physical illness that requires us to begin to reevaluate how we care for, nourish, and understand ourselves. By healing our bodies, minds, and spirits, we open the door to new levels of consciousness and next-level living.

We do not heal through speaking to the mind and convincing it of science, focusing solely on the cells and organs of the body. We heal holistically by opening the door to a much more profound and ancient understanding of what it means to be human. Healing unfolds by understanding the ultimate foundation of your body, emotions, thoughts, and spirit—by discovering the energy that you are in truth: your soul frequency. So relax, breathe, and open up to all that this book has to offer to not only lighten your body, but to enlighten your life. Here we go; let's do this!

Introduction

When I am at the end of my life, I will look back with the knowledge that I lived half of mine asleep and the rest of it awake. Reflecting back on it now, it almost feels like two different lifetimes, one spent wrapped up in non-sense and the other spent dismantling the non-sense and uncovering my inner truth. I spent most of the first half of life fixated on some idea of perfection, trying desperately to get somewhere, be something, do something, attain something, and other fruitless endeavors. I was obsessed with chocolate chip cookies to the point of addiction and never met a carb or a dessert I didn't love a little too much. I felt betrayed by my body and was never the "right" weight, at times turning to drugs to ease the pain. I grew more depressed and spiritually disconnected, which as you can imagine was a really big downer.

Behind the outward laughs, the good times displayed on social media, and the many wild things I did and still lived to tell, I was pretty lost on the inside and acting overly confident on the outside. The bottom line is that I didn't know who I was and wasn't sure how to figure that out until I had a profound experience that caused me to wake up and realize that an entirely new way of life was possible.

I was born a sensitive child. Sensitive meaning I saw and experienced other dimensions. It seems weird to write; I am not sure I have entirely wrapped my head around it, but my heart understands it. I had not talked much about it to many people until I decided to write a book for everyone to see, so I guess the cat's out of the bag: this was my reality. Those around me graciously tolerated what they did not understand, and the only person who really got it was my rose-quartz-crystal-wearing and deeply spiritual maternal grandmother, Dorothy. I imagine it was inconvenient for those I love to come home after a long day at work and head over to sit down on the couch, only to have their small child yell "STOP!" because they were about to sit on one of her two spirit friends. Our household was the making for a modern day sitcom.

Eventually, my deep desire to fit in and be "normal" clouded over my connection to spirit, and the childlike curiosity and openness that I was born with gave way to looking around for validation. Slowly and steadily, the pure essence of who I really was as a young girl was replaced by a growing addiction to people-pleasing, perfectionism, and eventually workaholism. I grasped for any semblance of external control, while balancing on uncomfortable high heel shoes.

Introduction

After years of living a life that garnered a lot of external praise but left me feeling empty inside, this contradiction took its toll on me physically, emotionally, and mentally. Being stressed out, black circles kind of tired, catching colds if there was a sick person within city limits, not to mention the weight... well it was not about to give up residence on the lower half of my body. One day my body simply gave in to the years of unhealthiness, and a diagnosis of skin cancer stopped me in my tracks. The word "cancer" uttered from the mouth of my doctor was no laughing matter. I was going to have a scar down the bridge of my nose forever; a scar that symbolized how long I had ignored my body and my spirit. A reminder that I kept running in circles when I should have stopped and listened to my inner voice gently whispering to me to re-evaluate, re-define, and re-connect.

I kept running in circles when I should have stopped and listened to my inner voice gently whispering to me to re-evaluate, re-define, and re-connect.

At the doorway to my 30s, in a desperate attempt to heal my body, I embarked on a journey of self-realization disguised as healthier eating; but what I had no way of knowing at the time is that in the eight years that would follow, I would end up transforming every perception I had about myself and reinventing truly every aspect of my life. Along this journey, I realized many things. The two most important of these discoveries were: one, that my lifelong preoccupation with weight and food was simply a distraction that kept me from acknowledging a much deeper disconnection; and two, that perfectionism was the strategy I used to find control over external circumstances, because the interior of my life felt utterly out of control.

Through almost a decade of study and research in nutritional science, psychology, and energetic healing, I came to understand that if we address physical imbalance at a purely superficial level through diet, surgery, etc., without diving into the emotional and energetic causes of these imbalances, we can spend a lifetime chasing an external ideal of "healthy" and never really find what inside we are so desperately seeking.

By the time the Big 4-0 was around the corner, I could no longer deny that the fairytale life I had worked so hard to create—consisting of the "perfect" career, marriage, home and family—looked bright and shiny on the outside, but some aspects of it felt like a bowl of sour cherries on the inside. Yes, everyone wants to put their best foot forward; but trying to show up in the world only presenting the "good" parts of ourselves often means becoming overly focused on things like cars, cabinet colors, tabloid magazines, the finest clothes, the latest episodes, our French manicures, and other soul-sucking fixations.

Introduction

When you are keeping up with the Kardashians, life becomes very exhausting and not so fulfilling. The marketing powers that be are great at spinning people's heads so they stay disconnected from their hearts. Beneath all of the fixations is a pressure cooker of emotions building up and ready to go Mount Vesuvius—until the first glass of wine or a piece of chocolate simmers the lava. The only way to truly save ourselves from this eruption is to dive into the blue waters and go deep within.

The marketing powers that be are great at spinning people's heads so they stay disconnected from their hearts.

As I began to heal and to honor and integrate all of the pieces of myself I previously did not acknowledge or accept, I came to understand what I now refer to as "the anatomy of transformation," which is comprised of four distinct phases: truth, release, experience, and align. I have since guided hundreds of women through these phases. The clients with whom I work seek me out for support in dealing with all kinds of conditions, ranging from low energy or weight gain, to wanting a new relationship, career, or whole life. But regardless of the diagnosis or each woman's goals, my intention is always the same. In my private practice and in this book, my sole purpose is to wake you up to who you really are.

It's time to jump out of hibernation, to start becoming fully alive and take some new and much-needed self-loving actions. One of the most effective ways to jump-start this process is to clean out your human vehicle. Years of eating chemicals disguised as food, breathing toxic air, and living in a state of dehydration keeps us dull. If we are going to sparkle and be lit up from the inside out, our bodies need to be clean and clear so more energy and light can course through. This light will bring along all-powerful creative energy that will expand our consciousness.

The truth is,
you are energy and light;
glorious, radiant, and powerful.

Not one other person on the planet has the same exact energy that you do, and by the time you are done reading this book, you are going to see just how magical you are. I call this unique, one-and-only rock star energy your "*soul frequency*." We are each born with a unique creative energy flow running through our bodies, and when we discover this force and learn how to align with it, we deepen how we experience life. We become receptive to streams of wisdom and inspiration we never have known before. It is next-level, off-planet kind of living. Our unique gifts come out of hiding and people start showing up to help us manifest what we are meant to create. And, in the process of living our own truth, we help others to find theirs, and to align with their soul frequency as well. We are all here to heal our minds and bodies so we can become fully, spiritually alive.

This book will guide you to become reacquainted with the part of you that is dying to be heard and reconnected to your unique soul frequency.

This book will guide you to become reacquainted with the part of you that is dying to be heard and reconnected to your unique soul frequency. It is a process of uncovering the truth of your deepest soul callings; of releasing the icky perceptions, beliefs, habits, stories, and self-concepts that are out of alignment with this truth; of tapping into your innate power to create the experiences you most want to have in this lifetime; and lastly of aligning every aspect of your life to support the highest expression and expansion of your soul. We are going to go deep, and laugh along the way. ☺

Throughout this book, I will share things that are deeply personal. I will put words to things that I feel are valuable on your journey. I offer my own personal experiences in the hopes that reading them will help you locate yourself in your own anatomy of transformation, and be reassured by knowing that someone really gets it, even if everyone around you thinks you have lost it or are having an inner crisis. From my own stories, and the stories of my clients, I hope you will feel how deeply you are supported and that you are not alone. Whatever degree of disconnection or dis-ease you are experiencing now or have experienced in the past is in fact a messenger summoning you toward your true purpose: to reunite you with the inner voice that resounded so clearly within you when you were a child, but has grown fainter over time. This voice, and the wisdom it brings, is a divine messenger sent to lead you back home to you. I have the honor of serving as your personal tour guide, making sure you keep your hands inside the car at all times and pointing out attractions along the route.

My guess is that you picked this book up

because it spoke to you in some way, because certainly no one on God's green earth knows what a soul frequency is until you dive right in and discover that it is exactly what you have been looking for all along.

Introduction

My guess is that you picked this book up because it spoke to you in some way, because certainly no one on God's green earth knows what a soul frequency is until they dive right in and discover that it is exactly what they have been looking for all along. Maybe you are seeking some insight into or relief from an unwanted physical condition or emotional pain. Perhaps you, like me all those years, are just hoping to lose some weight or feel better in your body. If this is your quest, know that you have been guided to the perfect place. Finding balance and lightness in your body and feeling overall healthier is a beautiful side effect of the process you're about to undertake; but the real transformation occurs when you begin to discover things about yourself that you didn't even know you were looking for.

Right now, at the outset of this journey, you cannot even fathom all the ways you are going to evolve and expand, or the many insights that will open up for you along the way. It's a bit like waiting for the checkered flag before the biggest race of your life. But as your body purifies, stabilizes, and realigns, you will create space for the dawning of a deeper truth. And if you follow this truth, you will find the pot of gold at the end of the rainbow; or even better, you'll come to realize that you *are* it.

SECTION I

Truth

Truth

Don't worry. I am not going to bore you with exhaustive scientific studies, nor am I going to give you an exacting meal plan that you have to follow in order to feel healthier, lose weight, or lighten your body. I'm not going to try to sell you on a particular brand of meditation or tell you about the latest treatments for curing any specific ailment. And yet, I *am* going to guide you through a very effective process for restoring energetic balance to your body and life, which is exactly how you get the things you want and keep them for the long-term. You will learn how to reignite the clarity, light, and life force energy in every aspect of your being.

You see, this book is founded on a central premise that you must accept—or at least consider as a possibility—before you can benefit from its powerful message: you are, at your core, whole, completely pure, positive energy. Yes, you are also flesh, blood, bone, atoms, cells, and molecules;

but the physical aspect of you has an equally important non-physical counterpart. This is the source of life, of radiance, of creativity, and inspiration. Whether you refer to this aspect of yourself as God, life force, spirit, soul, vibration, Mother Nature, or Obi-Wan Kenobi, this vital energy is the essence of you. It is your original soul frequency, which is now manifested in human form.

Your soul frequency is never depressed, anxious, insecure, negative, sad, unhealthy, or overweight. So, if you are currently identifying with any of those labels, the good news is that they are the not the real you. Regardless of the current state of your body or your mind—whether you're feeling bright and flexible or dull and uninspired—your soul frequency is the truth of who you are and is waiting to be awakened and utilized in every moment. Learning to discover this subtle rock-star essence and becoming increasingly willing to listen to it, trust it, and ultimately allow it to guide the unfolding of your life, is the plain and simple path to happiness, a sense of purpose, and glowing health.

It's All About Energy

The human body rocks. Seriously, it is brilliantly designed and made up of a trillion intricate and interconnected systems that enable it to function. But, if you were to place your body under a high-powered microscope, you would discover that the organs, tissues, cells, molecules, and sub-atomic particles that work together in such beautiful collaboration are neither solid nor static. They are in fact a sea of energy that is constantly moving and ever-changing. Nothing inside of you is standing still. Everything is dancing to the music of life.

Energy is the foundation of the human body and of everything that appears material and solid, including the book you are holding in your hands, the chair you are sitting on, the ugly holiday sweater that you got as a child, your favorite handbag, and even the thoughts you think. At every moment within your human form, physical, emotional, and mental energy is continuously flowing, and all of it is vibrating at a particular frequency. In other words, you, my dear, are a human symphony.

There is a vibe to everything and you either resonate with it or you are repelled by it.

Everything in the physical world has its own vibrational frequency—plants, rocks, family members, a parking ticket, and, of course, your omnipotent thoughts, ideas, memories, and emotions. There is a vibe to everything and you either resonate with it or you are repelled by it. In the same way different radio signals come into range by adjusting a radio dial, we experience different realities as a result of how we tune our energetic frequency. Imagine if you knew precisely how to turn this internal dial in such a way as to completely reinvent and rejuvenate the parts of your life that feel stagnant or lackluster? Well, the truth is that you do have this power. We all do. Because it's the quality of the energy that courses through us in body and mind that dictates our experience of life.

Now, when you think about the concept of energy, you may be thinking in old school terms like caloric energy or the energy it takes to run five miles. But what I want to engage you in here is a "new school" energy conversation. This understanding is by far the most powerful tool you have in your belt, and it's quite possible that you forgot you even put it there.

The fundamental rule in quantum science is that you can't observe the world as it is because observation changes the molecular structure of reality.

The main reason that conversations about this all-powerful energy have ever been labeled as "out there" or "woo woo" is to keep us from discovering just how magical we are. But the magic I will be referring to throughout this book is actually science—one of the most exciting branches of science that's emerged to date, in fact—and it's called quantum physics. Quantum physics has been studied since the early 1900s through the work of Max Planck, Albert Einstein, and Niels Bohr. It holds the single best theory of the universe. The fundamental rule is that you can't observe the world "as it is" because the act of observation changes the molecular structure of reality. So, when we look at something—simply by virtue of looking at it—it changes. It's enough to make the human brain go wild!

Come on a journey down a rabbit hole with me. You will want to read this little section a few times to let it sink in and no problem if the mind tunes it out because your consciousness is eating this up.

Quantum mechanics tells us that an electron (a sub atomic particle in an atom) is both a particle and a wave. There's a field for every known particle (that is a lot of fields 'cause there are a whole lot of particles), and, for each of them, the thing that we perceive to be a particle is just a localized vibration of that field. We supply energy to the field in particle collisions, causing them to vibrate. When we hear that "new matter" has been discovered, this means that we've caused the field to vibrate and are now observing the resulting vibrations. Literally nothing is solid, including you and everything around you. It's strange to realize that everything that has ever been created is because someone supplied energy to a field, creating particle collisions that caused the fields to vibrate. And the things we deem to be real are the resulting vibrations around us.

Let's be honest. The human brain hates the quantum world of small matter because the linear mind wants that electron to be solid and to know the exact location of it. Is it in front of me? Is it beside me? After all, if observation makes it appear to change positions, where is that darn electron in truth? We desperately want to pin down an answer, and yet, there is no fixed position for an electron. How annoying! This inspires many left-brain thinkers to label this phenomenon as "woo-woo," because if the five senses can't make sense of something, it's deemed impossible or "supernatural." The mind holds a strong view of what should be. The leap that is hard to make is that an electron does not actually pop into existence but is simply a probability cloud that shows you how likely it is that you will see the cloud.

So, what exactly does all of this brain-confusing information have to do with your life, your body, and the choices you make each and every day?

This little dance down the quantum rabbit hole gives you permission to loosen your grip on the reality you are currently living in and realize that reality is highly subjective and always in motion. What you supply energy to will vibrate and create new things, new ideas, and new realities, which is so beyond cool because it means that you are the powerful creator of your reality.

This is great news, since many of us feel powerless to create the body and the life we want. Embracing the quantum allows us to deem these limitations as what they are—invisible, baseless claims.

Understanding that we are always creating our reality helps us realize that by taking the right kind of action, we have the power to manifest our true desires. I'm not talking about the action that leaves you feeling drained, like getting up every day to battle traffic on the way to a job that sucks the life out of you. I'm talking the kind of natural, flowing, inspired action that is a result of following your intuition. It comes from beginning to create the life that you came here to live, at a frequency that feels best to you.

What you supply energy to will vibrate and create *new things, new ideas, and new realities.*

Much of this world runs on various forms of suppression designed to keep us thinking very small and not seeing beyond the five senses, the powers that be are not really interested in us waking up to discover our own energetic superpowers. Profits over people, hierarchy over community, and control over cooperation is a paradigm that is slowly losing its grip; but not without great resistance. Quantum science shows us that everything is a vibration of a field. You can either vibrate the fields of an old paradigm or direct your energy powerfully towards the creation of a new one. Understanding that you create your own reality, or that a particle is actually a wave and there is no true location for an electron is exactly the way you create anything—including the life and body that you want. In this book, I am going to let you in on ancient wisdom that will bring the quantum world right down to earth so your mind can learn to love it, use it, and create with it.

Thankfully, people like us are waking up and stepping up as a collective to understand that our only true power resides within us. When we learn to direct our energy on purpose, we can use it to create what we want, including a healthy body and mind. Once you learn how to raise the frequency of your own energy field and stand in your own power, the world is your oyster.

Now, before your fears and considerations are activated and begin to derail this conversation, I invite you to sit with this idea and allow it to expand what is possible for you. It is often way harder for people to envision that they can have everything their hearts desire than it is to accept feeling stuck or living in lack or limitation. This is painfully sad, but so true. And that is why we are going to squash this archaic mindset right now.

The truth about understanding energy is that it's not an intellectual process, but an experience that has to be felt.

The truth about understanding energy is that it's not an intellectual process, but an experience that has to be felt. We have got to get out of our heads and into our hearts; out of the nosebleeds and onto center stage in our life experience.

Learning how to expand the energetics of my body by feeding it high frequency fuel is what spontaneously blew open the door to my own healing and to the healing work that I now facilitate with others. Once you understand energy as I describe it throughout this book, your experience of reality will be forever changed. You'll become healthier in every sense of the word. Hang on to your hat, because what is about to ensue is literally one of the most insanely cool discovery processes of your life!

There are an infinite number of ways to experience and understand energy, so I encourage you to feel it out and find what resonates with you. It is my hope that this book will help you locate and expand your own signature soul frequency, that unique rock star energy that is the very essence of you. Energy begins to move when we start taking inspired action, and throughout this book you will have the chance to do your own inner work and unleash your magnetic energy. Do your best to *feel* the words you will be reading in your heart, and notice what awakens inside of you. Sometimes the very act of taking in someone else's life experiences, as you will do throughout this book, can ignite a new awareness within ourselves that burns brightly.

On these pages, you may find answers to many of the questions bubbling up in your own life, such as: How do I heal my body or lose weight? How can I find my purpose? How do I switch careers to something I enjoy? How do I find my soul mate? How do I achieve my goals? As you devour the pages of this book you may discover the answers to your burning questions and gain access to the most courageous parts of yourself. I encourage you to be open-hearted and open-minded and see what shows up as we go deeper into understanding the energy of our thoughts, emotions and our physical body. Speaking of our amazing beautiful bodies, let's learn how to better love, protect, and heal them.

Next-Level Healing

Apart from a handful of cutting-edge (and exciting) exceptions, we live in a world that still approaches the physical body, health care, and weight management in a way that leaves people feeling lost, questioning themselves, and putting their full trust in doctors that may not have all of the information. Most traditional practices of medicine are focused almost exclusively on managing sickness rather than keeping people well. We mask the symptoms of illness while failing to get to the root cause—and, maybe you've noticed: the root cause is never just physical. The body is not its own entity that is separate unto itself. It is an integral part of a brilliant and intricate communication system made up of the physical, mental, emotional, and spiritual aspects of ourselves. The state of one greatly affects all others. Everything is energy and it is all interconnected. In this never-ending feedback loop, negative thoughts trigger negative emotions, which cause stress, tension, or actual pain (you'll hear much more about how precisely this occurs in Section III).

To heal at any level of our being, we have to get real and start considering every aspect of self. To think of yourself in only the physical sense is archaic. Your body is only the very tip of a huge, expansive, energetic iceberg, and thankfully some healing modalities are now beginning to acknowledge this. There is a rapidly expanding sector of medicine known as psychoneuroimmunology, a branch of medicine that explores the influence of emotional states (such as stress) and nervous system functions on the immune system—especially in relation to the onset and progression of disease. What these researchers and scientists are proving is that our emotional states profoundly affect our immune system, and we've known for a long time that every disease begins as a result of a dysfunction in our immune system.

Energy Psychology is another mind-body approach that focuses on the relationship between bioenergy systems, neuro- and electro-physiological processes, and the mental functions that drive our thoughts, emotions, sensations, and behaviors. This area of study confirms that emotional triggers often underlie and contribute to physical ailments such as back pain, knee pain, hip pain, and even diseases as complex as cancer. The time has come to look at physical ailments as the signaling system to dive deeper into the mental, emotional, and spiritual aspects of overall health and healing, because the narrow scope of mainstream, "modern" medicine is simply not providing all the information we need to prevent illness and maintain vibrant health.

Gone are the days that we should be driving around town consulting a different doctor for each of our different ailments, without at least questioning the possibility that some of those ailments may have the same root cause. Visiting a psychologist to help us sort through our emotional problems, a physical therapist to alleviate joint or muscle pain, and a GI doc for symptoms such as heartburn or IBS may all prove helpful; but does this piecemeal approach really give us the full picture when we are dealing with an interconnected system? Each practitioner may be able to offer some incredible insight, but none has the benefit of seeing a 360-degree view of your inner and outer life, and this information is vital to understanding what is truly impeding healing. Add to this the fact that for the most part in standard Western medical care, doctors are overbooked. They spend less time with patients than ever before and their hands are increasingly becoming tied by insurance regulations. We are living in a time where we need to become our own advocates and develop enough self-awareness to seek out holistic practitioners who can provide information to help us connect the dots between our physical, mental, emotional, and spiritual states, so that we become more aware of what's actually happening in our bodies. We are not a collection of separate parts; we are holistic beings that are more intelligent, and with a greater capacity for self-healing, than most people understand.

It's ironic. We seem to acknowledge the concept of wholeness when it comes to mechanics, but not in relation to our own body. To repair any mechanical system—a conveyor belt, for example—you would first need to determine how each individual part is functioning in relation to every other part. And if you did discover a breakdown, you probably wouldn't take one piece over to one repairperson and another piece over to somebody else, because the efficiency of the machine as a whole relies upon the integration of all its individual parts. Plus, who has time to be driving all around town? We've got much better things to do.

We are not a collection of separate parts; we are holistic beings that are more intelligent, and with a greater capacity for self-healing, than most people understand.

Diseases are not isolated events, nor are they random or entirely genetic. They don't come "out of the blue." We can't accurately say we have trouble with our weight simply because our whole family does, or that we are sure we will end up with diabetes because everyone in our family has it. Dis-ease states originate at the level of energy and vibration. Our thoughts, emotions, life experiences, and actions play a significant role in any diagnosis. By the time we are experiencing a physical symptom, the imbalance has actually been going on for some time. This is ancient wisdom that is reflected in healing arts such as acupuncture, which works by inserting needles at particular meridian points in order to release blocked energy so that *chi*, or life force energy, can once again flow unobstructed through the body. Energy needs to move and when it gets stuck, illness ensues. To restore true balance, we have to look at what is impeding healing and stop popping pills, which only create more symptoms to mask. Masking symptoms is a losing battle and no way to live.

No More Band-Aids

Band-Aids are great for covering a wound, but they do not heal it. Only the body can do that. Today, we routinely apply Band-Aids over an ever-expanding list of symptoms, without a clue—or even a curiosity, it seems—as to understanding the source of them. We have a pill for just about anything and everything and they are being handed out like samples at the local candy store. We easily fall prey to "5 Days to Flatter Abs," cellulite cream, and insidious pharmaceutical commercials selling a nice bike ride by the lake—while they rattle off a list of unfortunate side effects including death.

Everywhere we look, there are people seeking to capitalize on our blind trust in a system that is broken. The diet industry alone is doing us a massive disservice by addressing weight gain and physical health in a way that not only doesn't work in the long-term, but actually separates us from our own intuition and sense of personal power. Sure, it's a money-maker that keeps people trying and buying, hoping this time will be different; but this approach is creating a population of people who have resigned themselves to a lifetime of diet after diet, a mountain of pills, and utter confusion about what is really healthy, which almost always leaves them with some sense of failure in the end.

In 2012, ABC reported a study that found that the average revenue of the weight loss industry is a staggering $20B per year, and that over 108 million Americans go on diets annually, with most making four or five attempts each year. The concept of "on a diet" then "off a diet," is rooted in failure, and we have to wonder how the yo-yo effect of perpetual dieting affects the psyche of those who buy into it year after year. How many people do you know who put themselves on a quickie weekend "detox" only to dive into a deep bowl of ice cream late Sunday evening? Or eat whole foods for thirty days, but can't wait for a glass of wine or two and pizza on the 31st day to celebrate?

It is awesome to eat well, and if we do it every day, the body will heal; but it can't heal without a consistent supply of the right macro-nutrients and micro-nutrients it needs. If we subscribe to eating well under the guise of a diet, then there is always an end date looming in the future. Right from the outset, our commitment to consistently eating healthy is standing on shaky ground.

Eating healthy and maintaining a weight that is comfortable to you is not a timed event.

Eating healthy and maintaining a weight that is comfortable to you is not a timed event. No one wants to achieve some fleeting ideal of success and as soon as the goal is reached, simply return to their old ways, gain back the weight, and be left feeling disappointed. In many cases, the underlying cause of excess weight is directly tied to being accepted and worthy of love. Dieting is a Band-Aid that covers this much deeper emotional wound. Of course, Band-Aids don't heal wounds, just like diets don't heal the reasons why we overeat.

Band-Aids don't heal wounds,

just like diets don't heal the reasons why we overeat.

You could say that food and I had a love/hate relationship. For most of my life, I was engaged in a constant battle with my weight, and while I was never obese—not even heavily overweight—the struggle was no less real. At only 5'1", even a little bit of extra weight was noticeable and felt like the end of the world to me.

We tend to tell ourselves that other people have it easier, like maybe being 5'1" and twenty pounds overweight seems like no big deal. But what I have come to realize is that it makes no difference how much weight one wants to lose and keep off; it's the mental anguish that accompanies this discrepancy that does a number on us.

For years, I went to extreme measures to control my weight—like eating crappy processed and toxic foods, living on diet soda and candy bars disguised as protein bars, fasting, taking diet pills, and eventually I turned to drugs to control my weight. I did a whole lot of destructive things in the pursuit of quieting my negative self-talk and attaining an exterior appearance that felt acceptable. If I could just keep the not-so-pretty painful stuff going on in my psyche hidden behind some slim fit designer jeans, a fresh highlight, and a smile, it felt like all would be A-OK.

Although I wasn't even present to this truth at the time and would never have uttered these words, so much of my worth as a woman was tied up in how I looked on the outside. I am cringing as I am writing this. Who wants to admit something like that? We live in a time of female empowerment, yet the subtle shackles of being slaves to our outer appearance are still there. And the omnipresent marketing industry is acutely aware of this vulnerable underbelly. It feels so wrong to be focused on the exterior; but the truth is, I spent a lot of energy and time obsessing over it. If I ate relatively well, I felt amazing about myself. If I put on a few pounds, on the other hand, a dark cloud loomed over my days.

This unhealthy relationship with food didn't just happen out of blue. I don't attribute it to my genetics and it wasn't simply because of the cookies that I loved. It was all of the emotions I had stuffed away for so many years, and the mean voice in my head that kept me in a vicious cycle of self-deprecation that was buried so deep, I was barely conscious that it existed. These two things—repressed emotions and the critical voice that tries to convince you that you are in some way flawed– have the power to tie up the flow of energy through your body like a Los Angeles traffic jam on a Friday night.

The excess weight
was only a visible symptom of the long repressed emotions and mental anguish that loomed beneath the surface.

Since I didn't realize I was living in this state of internal gridlock and had no understanding of how to express and release energy safely, food was a convenient distraction. I didn't have to experience the truth of what I was really thinking and feeling. The excess weight was only a visible symptom of the long repressed emotions and mental anguish that loomed beneath the surface.

In the many years that have passed since making this self-discovery, I have guided hundreds of clients toward a similar awareness and helped them to free themselves from the unconscious mental and emotional blocks that are at the heart of any unhealthy relationship with food. Here's a quick case-in-point:

By the time she came to see me, Caitlin had already consulted with a host of practitioners from Western MDs to naturopaths and DOs. The sheer number of doctors she'd seen led me to believe Caitlin had spent most of the past few months in the waiting rooms of medical offices. She had severe stomach issues and could barely eat without it causing her pain. She had been diagnosed with severe IBS and had a cabinet full of prescriptions and supplements, along with specific diet recommendations to follow. As we talked, Caitlin went on to tell me that she often forgets to take the supplements and rarely follows the dietary recommendations prescribed to her. I explained that this is actually quite common when healing needs to take place on another plane before physical healing is possible. It was clear that the root of her pain did not stem from the physical.

From the moment Caitlin walked into my office, I could feel that something was bothering her deep inside. A wonderful client had referred her to me, but still she seemed quite apprehensive about coming in for a consultation. In my work, I find that sometimes we fear a solution more than we fear feeling sick. Convinced that the devil we know is better than the devil we don't know, we avoid the truth; and yet, that is the very thing that will set us free from the pain.

After Caitlin spent most of our first session sharing about her life experiences, I suggested that she had been cut off from her personal power for years. I pointed out that her stomach pain was right where her third chakra is located, and explained that the third chakra (solar plexus) signifies self-worth, self-esteem, and one's innate power to choose. It turns out, these inner connections were in fact playing out in her outer life. While she had felt very powerful when she was younger, she had given up her power to the man she married ten years ago, and felt as though she no longer had a voice. Her stomach pain was indicative of the turmoil she was experiencing in relation to sacrificing herself to gain the love of another.

Over the few months we worked together, Caitlin began to speak up and take back her power, slowly and in her own time. Once we began to address this unconscious part of her that needed healing, she no longer felt resistant to foods that could support her body. Her stomach began to heal. Resistance always arises as a means to protect something unconscious, that when revealed clears the path for true healing. Once you understand that all manifestations of dis-ease—in body or in mind—are the result of a gradual covering of the vibrant light that we are at our essence, it becomes clear that the first step in reconnecting with our soul frequency must be to get real with ourselves about where in our lives we haven't been listening or honoring our own truth.

Inspired Action

- What negative thought patterns might be affecting your body, weight, and health?
- What emotional experiences have you not fully expressed or healed?
- As you read the remainder of this section, begin to make an inventory of what parts of your body and mind might be "crying out" for things to change.

Truth Heals

Regardless of how many mental gyrations or justifications are going on in the mind, the body knows the truth. It knows if you have veered far off track and it is always trying to bring you back into balance. The truth is that we rarely choose to seek better health or look within unless we have experienced some pain in regard to our weight, health, or some other crisis that impacts our life. So, realize that whatever physical, mental, or emotional pain is currently present for you, the first important phase in your transformation is to locate your truth. As you acknowledge what is really true for you and begin digging deep into the areas of you-ness that you may have previously abandoned, many small shifts may begin to occur. Upon this awakening, you may find yourself no longer interested in buying the tabloid magazine and instead reaching for your laptop to find healthier alternatives to your favorite foods. You may find yourself looking at the people in your life in a new way and asking yourself if they still "feel" good to you. You may start saying no to flashy events while you seek solitude within. These subtle inner stirrings and shifts are actually messages leading you in the direction of a more honest and authentic way of living that more closely resonates with your deeper truth. They are what I call "soul callings."

Ring, Ring, Ring!

Good Morning, Sunshine! It's time to wake up. Your soul has been calling you toward a bigger expression of yourself and now, out of courtesy, it is gently knocking at your door. You may experience this as inner-knowing, a little niggling, or the discontent you feel when you intuitively sense there is something more—some new possibility for yourself and your life that you may have never before allowed yourself to consider.

Soul callings often arise as a feeling of being somewhat restless or agitated and not quite knowing why. They are so quiet in the beginning that most people can easily eat, drink, dance, or shop them away. But as it gets louder, the call of the soul inevitably makes itself known through one or more of these common life experiences:

- The career you used to enjoy is now less than fulfilling.
- The relationship that used to center around senseless arguments, cocktails, and a superficial connection is now not so interesting or entertaining.
- The heavy indulgence in eating, snacking, smoking, or drinking is becoming a glaring issue.
- You find yourself wishing you could say "no" to people who suck the energy and life out of you.
- You've developed a fascination with things such as crystals, aromatherapy, or ancient healing techniques, and find yourself reading books like this one, about holistic health, consciousness, creativity, and living a fulfilled life.

- You're forming connections with new friends or colleagues who you describe as having a great "vibe," or find yourself dreaming about having new positive friends who inspire, support, and "get" you.

- You are becoming interested in new subjects, new people, and experiencing yourself as being more open-minded than ever before.

- You've recently experienced something that rattled you to your core, such as a death in the family, a break up, being fired, or the loss of a friendship.

- You are seeking a feeling of freedom from the hustle and bustle of life—the desire to be amongst the trees, maybe, to sit on a hilltop, or even travel the country in an RV.

- You feel like your life no longer fits like a glove. You desire something different, but may not be sure what that entails, and you may be experiencing a certain level of fear or anxiety about it.

When your soul comes a-callin', it feels like life is suddenly pulling you in a different direction. There is a feeling of movement about you; a sense that changes are around the corner, beginning with the way you think and feel about yourself and your life. At first, you may want to ignore it, and you may brush it aside time and time again. But eventually, if left unheeded, the call of your inner truth gets louder until change is banging down your door.

When the Truth Gets Loud

The call of the soul is the voice of your own inner truth. Whether it shows up as a desire to live a healthier life, begin a new career, create a new or improved relationship, a different living situation, or a sudden desire to clean out your closet, give up gossiping, or take a yoga class, you have a fundamental choice to make in the way you respond. You can choose to listen, trust, and allow yourself to go in the direction of where you are being led, or you can resist it and keep running into the same wall. The call of the soul has everything to do with regaining balance and improving your physical, mental, and emotional health. Continuing to ignore or hide from your inconvenient truths may seem like the path of least resistance and yet, it will eventually negatively affect every aspect of your life.

These pains are spiritual wake-up calls.

If you resist the call of your soul, symptoms of that resistance start manifesting: a growing shopping addiction, a few more glasses of wine, an extra fifteen pounds that won't budge, a mysterious back pain, or exhaustion like you have never felt before—or it may present as depression, anxiety, deep sadness, a loss of interest in life, or sudden bursts of sadness or anger. These pains are spiritual wake-up calls. Their purpose is to interrupt the status quo and support us in getting off the bleachers and onto the court of our own lives in order to stretch beyond our current limitations and into our full potential. Soul callings are usually very uncomfortable, because if they were comfortable we would just keep snoozing our way through life. They force us outside of our comfort zone.

Prepare to be totally unprepared to take the steps that you are being called to take. If you do not feel some degree of fear, doubt, and distrust in self, then it is not a soul calling. Almost nobody fully trusts themselves, and soul callings provide a fertile opportunity to build self-trust by first having the experience of completely doubting yourself. Whether you follow willingly or go kicking and screaming, you are nevertheless being pulled towards a deeper relationship with your true self. Oftentimes we don't listen to the call because we are holding on for dear life to the things that are no longer meant for us; but like everything in life, we have a choice about how we ride out this transformational experience. Do you surf with the waves or let them throw you against the rocks?

Right now, you might be thinking, *I don't care about my soul frequency, unearthing my truth, or living a more fulfilled life. I just want to lose weight, or feel better in my body. I just want to silence the ugly voice in my head or stop feeling so tired and run down.* The sub-text here is "get me out of pain, now." And yet, the solution and freedom we crave can only ever be gained by going within, beneath the pain, right back to where it all began.

Inspired Action

- What is a truth that you are afraid to share?

- Where are you or others in your life not honoring your truth?

- What is a truth that you are holding on to that you fear will be too inconvenient for yourself or others if you were to speak it?

- When and with whom is it hardest for you to tell the truth?

- See if you can allow yourself to acknowledge a piece of your truth here and now, within the safety of these pages and the sacredness of this process.

The First Disconnect

We are all lost on some level and we don't even know it. Most of us have clouded over the ability to access what is really true for us because we have been trained from early on to prioritize other people's perceptions, needs, and opinions above our own. We love Broadway plays like our mom, we dream of having as many kids as we had in our family of origin, and we cheer for our father's favorite soccer team, whether we understand the game or not. As souls, we arrive in a human body as pure potential and with a full connection to our soul frequency. We are born without judgments, filters, and beliefs; but as we enter a family system made up of people who have plenty of their own belief systems, opinions, and ideas about life—especially about whom they want their children to be—we can't help but take some of that on.

To stray too far from the expectations or approval of our caretakers is to risk death, so we conform instead.

As infants, our survival is completely dependent on our caretakers, and we need to be accepted to make sure we get clothed and fed. It may sound primal, but at the end of the day we are animals and those who fit in the best have the greatest chance at survival. As children, we are extremely sensitive to everything and everyone in our environment. As we grow, we begin to learn what life is and how to approach it by watching the adults in our midst. If we are going to survive as baby tigers, we better stick close to the den and mind our parents, or they just might let us starve.

We learn early on that it's not safe to run around making a lot of noise when mother is angry, or to make special requests at the end of a long day when dad is tired. The moral of the story is, stay on the good side of the people who feed you. This imperative is hardwired into our DNA. To stray too far from the expectations or approval of our caretakers is to risk death, so we conform instead. Our decision to conform may have been unconscious and instinctual, but we made it all the same. Often this fear-based primal instinct is at the expense of being happy, authentic, and fully self-expressed. It takes deep self-awareness for adults to view their children as unique souls that come forth with great wisdom that may differ from their own, and it takes courage to honor these differences. While my own family system carried on in what seemed to be a very typical middle class suburban lifestyle, we each had different personalities, saw life in different ways, and ultimately had different soul missions to fulfill.

My dad was an adventurous, type A, life-of-the-party, football coach turned successful real estate broker. Everything he touched turned to gold. My mother was book smart, kind, and worked as a teacher. Of course, they are much more than a simple description, they had dreams, gifts and were incredible at many things. Bottom line, I loved both of them dearly and yet I felt very different compared to them. In my family a sense of duty was important, stress was commonplace, and using your mind was regarded as more valuable than listening to your heart. This is not an uncommon energetic familial archetype and it is neither bad nor good; these were simply the subtle overtones of energy in my home and one of the many familial archetypes that I typically see in my practice.

In my family, duty was valued over happiness, stress was far more commonplace than peace, and using your mind was regarded as far superior to listening to your heart.

Some of my first memories were of feeling alone—not physically, but emotionally. The experience of feeling lonely when we're surrounded by people is confusing, which causes us to question ourselves. Logic tells us it is impossible to feel lonely in the presence of others; and yet, so many people do. I remember playing for hours by myself in my room at the back end of our small tract home, allowing my imagination to take me to far off lands. Looking back, the depth of human connection that I craved often came from a world beyond our three dimensional reality. The two very kind, playful, and reassuring spirits that ushered me into this life helped ease the loneliness of the human experience. I saw them, I spoke to them, and they kept me company. I experienced them fully without words. I felt that they knew me and I knew them. They were representatives of the world of energy and consciousness, and to me, they felt like home.

In my perception, there were five of us living in our house; but in actuality, there were only three. This created a huge chasm between the way my parents and I experienced life. They did the best they could to work around what they could not see, but I couldn't understand their blindness. In my reality, I saw spirits. I was extremely affected by the feelings of others and I wasn't sure what to make of the differences between our experiences.

Here it's important to note that not all children have experiences with spirits, but all of us experience energy.

Here it's important to note that not all children have experiences with spirits, but all of us experience energy. Long before we can talk, we read the pulse of our homes and integrate our findings into an archetype for what it means to have a human experience. Imprints are happening not only at the levels of seeing and hearing, but more powerfully at the levels of feeling and sensing. We are so much more than a human body, and we have got to start knowing this with every bio-photon that we are.

Anyway, once I became old enough to realize that the world around me was watching black and white TV while I was seeing life in Technicolor, I began to feel like I wasn't normal. "I'm not normal" was my First Disconnect, and would become a central decision that I made about myself many times throughout my life; but as a young child, I did my best to reverse the feeling of separation between my parents and me by shutting down everything that was unique about my human experience. I wanted to be like anyone other than myself.

By the age of five, I had finally succeeded at cutting off my connection with spirits, energy, and the unseen world. In the process, I lost my connection with my inner self. Life became centered around baby dolls, swim lessons, and—my favorite at the time—cupcakes, while my multidimensional truth was slowly buried underneath. It sucks to not feel understood. It is brutally painful to the point that most will opt to disconnect from self in an attempt to meld with those around them. At the end of the day, we all need to be "fed" and will do whatever is required to stop the hunger. Eventually, I decided the best chance I had at gaining the love and approval I so desired was to disconnect from all that makes me a unique soul, and to sign up for normalcy instead.

Inspired Action

- Write down a list of the major events you can remember in your life from ages five to ten years old.

  For each event, you likely formed a belief about yourself, your caretakers, or life as a whole.

  These core beliefs are often constructed in simple language that a child could convey and are very succinct. For example, a little boy on the playground makes a snide comment to a little girl about her face and in that moment she forms a belief, "I am ugly."

- What are the beliefs you may have formed as a result of the events of your childhood?

  The First Disconnect represents the core beliefs that you formed about yourself that separated you from knowing that you are whole, perfect, lovable, and complete.

I Want What You Want

Be gracious, be pleasant to others, and never make waves or make anyone else feel uncomfortable. Conform, contract, and for goodness sake, please smile while doing so, lest you give the impression of being less-than-grateful. This is at the basis of the unconscious programming that many people grow up with. I have seen various versions of the First Disconnect expressed countless times in private sessions with clients over the years. Each life story has its own unique nuances, and yet the common theme is almost always related to conforming to the ideals, beliefs, and constructs of others, rather than listening to one's own truth. Although this unconscious strategy may seem doable in the first part of our lives, burying ourselves under the needs of others will eventually suck the life out of us. However it plays out, the First Disconnect becomes a gateway to one of the most deadly diseases of all: people-pleasing.

From the age of five until I finally woke up to this pattern, I looked to other people for cues on what was cool and acceptable. I was concerned only with what I should be doing to gain attention and praise, and I could not have cared less about my truth buried so deep below the surface that it almost ceased to exist. Based on my own early imprinting, I came to the conclusion that fitting in was the most important thing to achieve in life, so this became my goal. I went about choosing activities based on the desires of others. Or at least, what I believed they would desire. I had this deep need to make people happy and to avoid feeling the intense energy of disappointment from others.

Even the slightest air of disapproval or indifference cut like a knife and jeopardized the chance at gaining more love and acceptance.

I had this deep need to make people happy and to avoid feeling the intense energy of disappointment from others.

Typically, parents are always trying to make the best decisions they know how to make in order to guide children in the direction they believe is healthy. But in most parent/child dynamics, it is often rare that parents can fully see beyond the veil of their own desires to recognize the child's unique soul mission and life experience. It takes profound awareness to create a safe space for children to cultivate their unique gifts. It is important to witness the true nature of a child and to allow them space to find their own rhythm and truth.

Children are unique and handle emotion, discord, and self-imposed or externally-imposed pressures in different ways. Some are able to brush things off. Some distract themselves with interests outside the home. Some children act out, while others become anxious and emotionally disconnect from what's happening around them. Some decide that it's not safe to speak up. As a child, I internalized.

Inspired Action

While you reflect back over your own childhood, notice if you—like me—developed the habit of toughening up in order to make others more comfortable. Did you tend to follow along with the expectations of others, mistaking them for your own? Or did you portray yourself as a rebel to those outside of you, all the while secretly longing for their understanding and acceptance?

- I challenge you to look at the one trait that made you different and begin to embrace the possibility that it is likely your greatest gift.

The sensitivity that I chalked up to being my biggest downfall is now my most precious resource and the very foundation of my life's work.

Separating From "the Pack"

There is an unwritten law in family systems that we don't speak out against the other members, that we must sacrifice ourselves to protect the whole, and that it's better to hold in our hurts than to risk hurting others by speaking them. And regardless of how normalized this mindset is in your family of origin, I must tell you, my friend, that giving into this type of human pack mentality is the fast track to feeling alone, unheard, addicted, and disconnected. To heal, we need to find our truth, feel it deeply, and then give it a voice. It takes a crazy amount of courage to be real when almost no one else wants to be. But if we keep holding in our feelings for the sake of pleasing or protecting others or ensuring our survival within the group, we will never experience true freedom. Freedom is born from finding the courage to speak our truth. We can spend years dancing around it, but getting real about our experiences is the most cathartic experience *ever.* Until we get real, we will remain stuck repeating the same patterns and creating the same unfulfilling experiences.

Just in case you haven't already noticed, people-pleasing leaves you empty, run down and exhausted. Not to mention that relying on the approval of others makes it all but impossible to make your own decisions with confidence. For those who think they're scoffing at the people-pleasers by donning a "devil may care" attitude towards everyone, please realize that this is actually the same energy in action, playing out on the other side of the spectrum. Whether we are people-pleasing or people-resisting, we are not at peace, nor are we living from our own personal power. When the fear of measuring up is driving our internal operating system we will never experience balance, autonomy, or equanimity.

Under these self-imposed conditions, we are highly susceptible to what I call the "snowball effect." It goes like this: disempowerment builds slowly beneath the surface, which is uncomfortable; so we cover it up with excessive eating, drinking, shopping, approval-seeking, having affairs, and so on. Over time, this self-created snowball grows in size—and then we add in the tension, depression, anxiety, and self-loathing that we accumulate as a result of partaking in these behaviors and the snowball becomes even bigger and faster. Then, in an attempt to stop the ball and to make sense of the self-sabotaging behaviors that result from our own disconnection from ourselves, we desperately look outside of us for help on how to stop the momentum. Yet, the answer lies inside of us. We'll turn just about anywhere, it seems, to avoid listening to our inner truth. We seek out the advice of doctors, healers, and friends. We scour the latest books for answers, all the while unaware that we were born with an inner compass, our own personal GPS that is trying desperately to flag us down and direct us towards our greatest purpose. What we really need is for people to lead us back to ourselves; to affirm that we have the strength and the ability to pay attention to *our* path and teach us how to hear the truth and not get derailed by sideshows.

Don't follow people for the sake of following people. Only seek people who help you truly listen to your truth. When we lose our connection with this inner compass and get caught up in the opinions of others, we feel as if we are in the middle of the desert without water, grasping frantically at every mirage that appears in the distance. Now, I would love to tell you that there is an easy answer that would allow you to skate right over the top of this; and yet, the only way out is by searching in the depths for your truth and wading through the murky waters as you learn to express it.

We'll turn just about anywhere, it seems, to avoid listening to our inner truth.

Inspired Action

- Where are you sacrificing your own happiness and fulfillment in order to make others happy?
- Where are you feeling a lack of clarity or self-expression?
- Do you have difficulty making decisions or moving forward in life?
- What are five areas where you could more directly verbalize your needs and begin taking back your power?

Pop the Lid

There is no sense trying to tap dance around the fact that life is freaking painful. Yes, it is joyful, awe-inspiring, and exciting too, but being human means we are going to experience pain in all forms. Usually, the very first painful events that we experience between birth and the age of about ten years old create the deepest imprints, shaping our personality and the way we view life, ourselves, and other people. Some children experience obviously tragic events, such as emotional, physical, or sexual abuse, the loss of a loved one, or their parents' divorce. However, there are also many children who live through experiences that, though apparently benign from an adult's perspective, are deeply tragic for the child. For example, being teased by other children at school, rivalry with a sibling, suffering a minor injury, internalizing hurtful comments made by teachers or parents, or experiencing fear and uncertainty as a result of a cross-country move. These seemingly inconsequential events can be just as devastating to the child who experienced them as are incidents that are more universally considered to be traumatic.

Let's be real. Many people grew up with parents who weren't exactly role models for the healthy expression of painful emotions—some parents were even strong advocates for repressing them. As a result, we are often more uncomfortable with emotion than we are standing in pointy toe pumps for eight hours straight. Many of us are fully unequipped to process and express the range of feelings we may experience during a traumatic event. But leaving these feelings unaddressed, shapes our future in many negative ways, ranging from slightly annoying to downright destructive. For example, a girl who is sexually abused at a young age may have difficulty trusting men later in life, while a boy who is teased in elementary school may become angry and combative as a young adult. These are just two illustrations of the ways that both overt and covert trauma can cause us as children to make core decisions about who we are and how we will interact with the world. Some of us will spend much of our lives trying to keep the lid on these painful emotions while others don't even know they are there. Either way, conscious or unconscious, those early decisions are at work beneath the surface of our awareness, silently running the show.

Some of us will spend much of our lives trying to keep the lid on these painful emotions while others don't even know they are there.

The most painful event in my life from birth until the age of ten was the divorce of my parents. By the time I was eight years old, my parents were like two ships passing in the night. I could feel the distance and the tension in my house, but I had become accustomed to it. First it was separate bedrooms. Then my father was moving out. The sadness was unbearable. What did this mean? What was life going to be like now? Would they be okay? Would I be okay??

For the next two years, our family waded through trial separations and reconciliations; but eventually the divorce proceedings began. My mom gathered her half of the belongings and we moved out of our family home and into a smaller house down the street. The day we moved, my heart shattered into a million pieces as I sat on the steps of what used to be my home feeling separated from any feeling of comfort and security. The rug had been pulled out from under me and the devastation was so deep that all I could feel was numb. I don't remember crying much. If there is a level beyond pain, I was there. At ten years old, I died a little.

At ten years old,
I died a little.

It was the first time I felt truly out of control. I had done nothing wrong and yet I felt like I got put in a time-out. I had to move out of my house, go days without seeing my dad, and everything that I had known about life thus far had suddenly changed.

For each person there is a tipping point when the pain becomes too great, and the door to our heart simply closes to protect us from further hurt. To ensure our own survival, we cut ourselves off from our feelings, and with that unconscious decision comes the birth of a coping mechanism. In my case, unable to understand these big feelings and feeling alone and devastated, I turned to the one thing that was always available in order to soothe my pain: food.

Inspired Action

- What or who has broken your heart in your past?

  Know that it is safe to look there: and that in fact, healing begins when we have the courage to look, feel, and understand the past. Sometimes our past hurts are not so obvious. So really ask yourself, *Where am I hurting or trying to avoid the pain?*

When Food Is Love

Food is not love, but it sure can feel like it. From the time we are very young, the Cocoa Puffs, potato chips, and cookies we develop intimate relationships with are closely associated with the emotion of love. We might have great memories of favorite holiday meals made with love by family members—our grandma's apple pie or our aunt's scalloped potatoes. We might have been given ice cream to soothe a skinned knee or to reward an "A" on a report card. Or you might remember getting special sweets at Disneyland, or looking forward to that bucket of buttery popcorn at the movies. Regardless of the context, our early memories around food often feel warm, loving, and soothing.

There are two primary reasons for overeating: we either want to avoid a person, a feeling, a memory, or experience in our lives; or we are missing a person, a feeling, a memory, or experience.

Once this first connection is made in the brain between a food (or any other substance) and the experience of love, pleasure, or the temporary relief of sadness or pain, a pattern is established. An emotion is felt when a particular food is eaten, and if this association continues, the desire to experience that emotion again will directly trigger a desire for that food. When bad stuff happens, we unconsciously make a beeline for these foods to soothe the pain and provide comfort. In doing this, we make a misguided attempt at regaining happiness.

Some people eat when they are hungry and stop when they are satiated—but many don't. The difference is in the way we relate to food and why we are turning to food in the first place. There are two primary reasons for overeating: we either want to avoid a person, a feeling, a memory, or experience in our lives; *or* we are missing a person, a feeling, a memory, or experience. Often, we have to dig deep within our hearts to uncover what is missing or what we are trying to avoid. Anytime we keep eating to the point that we are no longer listening to our body, it's a very good indicator that there is some emotional trigger or negative mindset that is stuck as energy in our bodies and needs to be released.

We are not a self-storage unit and we are not meant to accumulate years of emotional pain. In the same way your body can't house the record player from the '70s or Aunt Becky's tea set, it certainly has no room for all of the drama you have experienced over the past several decades, whether your own or inherited. We need to clean out our closet daily, deeply feel whatever comes up so we can move through and learn from it, and get rid of what no longer serves a purpose. There is a natural ebb and flow to pain. It is supposed to be felt and expressed fully. The aches and pains we typically chalk up as a sign of aging, bad luck, or stress, are often physical manifestations of repressed emotional pain. For many of the people I work with, there is a specific point in their lives—whether they remember it or not—where food became their go-to lid to keep emotional pain at bay, just as it did for me after my parents' divorce.

Once we were living in our little house down the street, my mom and I were getting through the shattering in the way most people do: you just pick up and keep on going, rolling right over the top of the pile of rubble like it isn't even there. Most women feel like their emotions are inconvenient (and who has time for them anyway?), which explains why we do things like hold in tears or leave a conversation in a huff instead of giving a voice to our anger. The biggest elephants in the room are usually people's repressed emotions, and we run from them like the plague. And if we haven't yet learned how to feel and process our feelings, most of us will instinctively try to purge that powerful energy from our bodies in a different way.

Think about the voracious housecleaning sessions you've initiated after a big argument, or the long run you take when that jerk at work is at it again. Since housecleaning and long runs weren't in the picture yet when I was ten years old, I began baking and discovered that I had a real affinity for desserts. My lid of choice to block the pain was chocolate chip cookies, preferably with a light crispiness on the outside and a gooey center. I was particular about my cookies like people are particular about their wine. Let's face it, being particular provides an outlet for even more of that misdirected emotional energy. I knew the recipe for chocolate chip cookies by heart. I became a master and I enjoyed eating them as much as I liked making them. And I was completely clueless as to the effect this new habit was having on my body. The lights were on, as they say, but I was not home.

Intense pain automatically sends us into survival mode. We are unable to access higher states of consciousness such as self-awareness or peace when we're focused on survival. Not only did I not realize why I was eating so much, I am not even sure I noticed the weight coming on little by little. This is how unconscious we become when we cut off our emotions in desperation to survive. Nevertheless, between the 5th and 6th grade, I gained twenty pounds. The stage had been set for years of struggle.

Inspired Action

- Do you turn to food when stressed, sad, disappointed, frustrated, tired, or feeling unfulfilled?
- Does food feel loving, comforting, or exciting?
- When did food feel like love as a child?
- When was food a reward?

Thick Wool Blankets

When we are experiencing pain and trauma in either body or mind, our fight-or-flight response is elevated, and our level of self-reflection is very low. All available blood rushes from our digestive tract to our limbs to help us outrun the imaginary lion. The issue these days is that most people are flipping the "Get Out of Dodge" switch while chowing down on a burger and fries, and this leaves the body in a state of massive confusion. We are not built to live riding our gas pedal continuously while unconsciously mowing down fake food. We need our brakes, which puts us into rest-and-digest, a state where the body can actually repair.

While we are mainlining caffeine, running from our emotions, and piling our calendar with more "to-dos," we are damaging our bodies and minds without even knowing it. The only way to feel and heal is to give ourselves time to stop. I would like to say that this "pedal to the metal" syndrome is rare, but it is more common than not. In fact, it is as standard as the plain black t-shirt that almost every single person owns. I see this degree of disconnection all the time in people of all ages and backgrounds. The trauma may have occurred years in the past; but in our attempt to block the pain, we keep running towards nowhere.

If you think holding in emotions at ten years old is tough, imagine being a sixteen year old in pain who doesn't want to feel. That is a recipe for disaster. In my case, by the time I reached sixteen, all of the emotional energy that had built up under the surface now had six additional years to simmer. Every day new hurts piled up and drove my food addiction to new heights. Clearly, I needed a bigger lid for this boiling pot. As human beings, we have an incredible capacity to adapt to things in order to continue suppressing the truth. The pain of life can get to the point where digesting it seems impossible, and the only way to keep it down is to keep adding more lids to the equation.

The trauma may have occurred years in the past; but in our attempt to block the pain, we keep running towards nowhere.

The teenage years and early twenties are not easy for anyone. By that time in anyone's life, they have experienced some real pain and for some, there are layers and layers of pain piled on like thick wool blankets. Heading into my teen years, the load of pain around my parents' divorce was already heavy. Pile on some young infatuation gone bad, your typical teenage fights with parents, and the feeling that I would never be free from my struggle with food, and it was like a chemistry experiment going awry. Using food to suppress the pain is awesome until you start gaining more and more weight and then it backfires and now you need something for the weight.

Enter, drugs.

Brilliant! I discovered drugs that both helped control my weight so I could still overeat without it showing on my body as well as had the added bonus of effectively making sure I felt as little as possible. A real winner! Except that the human psyche is very aware that none of these lids are truly taking the pain away. And so, it continues to look for another, bigger lid for this boiling pot. This is exactly how people end up with multiple addictions layered on top of each other and all of them are adding to, rather than solving, the problem. There is still pain and each lid creates more pain. The root of all addiction is unresolved emotional pain. Here is an example of how chasing lids to cover unwanted feelings manifests in some people's lives.

Kristin came to see me because she was gaining weight and wanted to make it stop. Through our first conversation, I learned that she was a huge fitness buff; but about a year ago she started having bad back pain, which just mysteriously showed up with no particular injury. After visiting with various practitioners to heal the physical pain, she was left with only short-term pain relief then it would return with a vengeance. It began affecting her daily life pretty quickly and soon she was unable to exercise. This was devastating for her and contributing to her weight gain. Since I know that weight is never about food, we talked on a deeper level about what was going on in her life. Over one conversation, it became clear that her pain was actually stemming from the stress of an unhappy marriage and events that had transpired between her and her husband.

She went on to share that she had begun drinking a glass of wine every evening to help with the back pain, which then became two glasses and then went up to three glasses of wine every night. As tears started to roll down her face, she went on to share that two weekends earlier, she had left her house in the evening to pick up a friend, rolled through a stop sign, and immediately saw the red and blue lights behind her. Kristin was pulled over, tested above the alcohol limit, and was arrested for DUI. My heart broke for her and the many people who are experiencing their own version of this scenario.

For most of Kristin's life, exercise provided a convenient lid for painful feelings. She would release energy through exercise, which is healthier than many other lids, but is still a lid. Eventually, she manifested pain in her back and alcohol became a second lid since the first lid was no longer available. This created the opportunity for a DUI. Through our work together, Kristin healed her physical body and her heart by moving through the emotions she felt towards her husband. She also developed a healthier way of exercising that allowed her to move her body without pain, and no longer needed the wine.

Lids are a severely ineffective coping mechanism

for unresolved pain that wreaks havoc on our bodies and our lives.

Lids are a severely ineffective coping mechanism for unresolved pain that wreaks havoc on our bodies and our lives. They end up creating devastation, divorce, breakups, loss of jobs, addiction, fear, disconnection, and a pile of other issues that can be difficult to unwind and heal. The more lids, the more unexpressed pain. In my opinion, we should stop teaching our kids silly subjects that no one ever remembers, worrying about their grades, and hoping they get accepted into the right college as a mark of a successful life, and start teaching them *Feeling Your Emotions 101* instead. Far more valuable than learning how to solve for X is knowing how to move through pain and develop the ability to allow emotions to flow out of us in a safe and healthy manner. Emotional literacy has the power to literally save people's lives and to end the constant chase for more lids. If it were taught in school, I assure you those kids would become the most resilient and successful adults on the planet.

Healing or lightening the body is a byproduct of knowing ourselves. If we want to have balanced weight and a healthy body, we have got to work through the tough stuff–not for the purpose of endlessly wallowing in it, and certainly not as an excuse for casting blame on others; but to give ourselves permission, finally, to let our emotions flow in a safe and healthy way without attaching meaning to them or using them to perpetuate drama. Instead of trying to run away from the past, we should be running towards it.

There is great power in being able to go back into our childhood to identify the significant events around which we may be still holding onto pain. Sometimes we may not have a conscious memory of these events right off the bat. Oftentimes, it takes a trusted professional to guide us to certain painful memories in a gentle manner. Whatever path you take, the journey is well worth it. Your personal power lies in your ability to become comfortable with the full range of your human emotions and be able to express them safely. This is the key to moving the stuck energy out of your body and to opening up to your full creative potential.

Inspired Action

- What are the lids you use to avoid feeling things that are scary, inconvenient, or uncomfortable?
- Make a list of the lids you use to cope in life, and place a check mark next to the ones that you want to stop doing today.
- Circle the ones that are harder to let go of and will take some inner work and focus to release.

Your Cravings Are Not the Real You

It's important to realize that whatever substance we are craving—be it food, alcohol, casual sex, drugs, or a new pair of shoes—we are seeking it because we truly believe that having it will make us feel better. The desire to feel better, to experience a bit of relief or happiness, is at the root of all our desires; but the truth is, we can never find true, sustainable happiness from any object outside ourselves. Happiness is the byproduct of knowing and honoring our inner truth, and being courageous enough to authentically express how we feel and who we are in the world. The voice in your head that wants to eat a whole pizza or drink a bottle of wine is not the real you. Every client I have ever worked with has her own favorite "go-to" craving. Some find it easy to eat healthier, but the thought of giving up wine seems impossible. Other women may not drink alcohol, but if you take away their evening chocolate fix, all hell will break loose. If you are not sure what your "go-to" lid is, just think about your favorite foods or drinks and imagine someone saying you can't have it. Look to the one that evokes anger or irritation.

There was a time in my life where if someone told me to give up chocolate chip cookies, I would have felt agitated and told them to mind their own freaking business. The thought of not having chocolate chip cookies felt horrible, like what is the point? Who would want to live that way? I had a huge energetic charge on my sweet, circular friends. After all, they had been there for me without fail every time I needed them. That is dedication, and I respected it! The underlying cause for cravings is twofold. One has to do with the part of your brain that you can think of as the "crave center." Not to get too technical, but this part of your brain lights up like a Christmas tree in the presence of sugar. So, if you routinely crave carbs, wine, alcohol, or sweets, it simply means that your crave center has got a round-the-clock party going on, disco ball and the full shebang.

Sugar sends off a bigger party in the brain than cocaine. It is the number one cause of a crave center party, and like most partiers, no one wants the fun to end, so the crave center is always urging you to have just one more bite. But it is not just sugar that can send you out of your house in your jammies on a high speed run; it may be a quesadilla, a burger, some fries, Thai food, or wine–(for the love of wine–why does she keep talking about wine?!)–or whatever tickles your fancy.

The second cause of cravings is the lids we just talked about that keep your emotions at bay. Cravings are nothing more than a brain party and a lid for your emotions. It can be one or the other–or for most people, it is a little of both. Each one promises a quick fix that never really fixes anything and never delivers any peace. Peace happens when we have the courage to take the lid off, stop the party, and see what comes.

Inspired Action

- What are your go-to cravings?

  Those pesky ones that are very hard, if not impossible, to say no to. It is always good to call them out and write them down in one place. That way they know you are on to them!

Change Your Food: Change Your Life

Food is the one addiction that no one can quit cold turkey. It is something we have to make peace with because we need it to survive. Most people don't understand how powerful a role healthy food plays; it not only helps heal the body, it also helps us access more self-awareness and allows more of our pure, positive energy to flow through us. Few of us were taught to think about food this way: as an access point to more creativity, more consciousness, and insight into who we really are; but this is precisely what opens up when we change the way we eat. With the right nourishment, you gain access to your own inner rock star: confident, cool, creative, and exuding a magnetic energy that draws people to you.

With the right nourishment, you gain access to your own inner rock star: confident, cool, creative, and exuding a magnetic energy that draws people to you.

When the body is full of icky toxins, our metabolism gets overloaded, our energy level diminishes, and our light—at every level of our being—becomes dimmed. These toxins can come in the form of pesticides, fungicides, and residue from improperly digested foods. They can also be chemicals in the home, air outside, or in water. And when the body is no longer able to filter out the influx of toxins moving through the system, it will actually start to create fat cells to store the toxins in an attempt to protect the body from harm. This is behind the "I keep gaining a few pounds every year even thought I eat the same" phenomenon.

In truth, our bodies are always trying to protect us from the toxic effect of physical pollutants, repressed emotions, or belief systems and mindsets that do not serve us. Your body is on your side and is your personal security team. Extra weight is stored personal power that is currently being used for our protection rather than our empowerment. By discovering the truth of what we are protecting ourselves against, we liberate the stored personal power that we have been blocking. When our focus is on reconnecting with our soul frequency and expressing it fully in the world, we stop focusing on weight, and it naturally falls away.

One of the most effective ways to keep someone disempowered is to feed him or her poor quality food, because in short time that person will likely become depressed, anxious, overweight, and tired, and no one can bring forth their best self when dealing with all of this. When we eat clean, organic foods that are close to nature, the body does not have to spend as much energy on digestion. This means we have energy for other things. Gently and over time, as we are able to clean out the toxins from tissues, organs, and cells, the body operates better, the mind operates better, and we gain access to more of our innate pure potential. The solution to losing weight is not another restrictive diet, because these don't work. The solution is discovering how to integrate healthy eating into your life, so it becomes a constant like brushing your teeth. No one forgets to brush his or her teeth for months on end (at least I hope not).

The key to success is bringing healthy eating into your lifestyle, not attempting to follow someone else's plan.

The key to success is bringing healthy eating into your lifestyle, not attempting to follow someone else's plan for a short period of time. It is not my intention with this particular book to go into detail about the healing effects of specific foods, but if you are interested in exploring this more fully, I highly recommend that you do so. Developing a thorough understanding of how nutrition can open up paths for you to access higher levels of consciousness, enable more lightness and energetic flow in your body, find and maintain a healthy weight, and have lots more physical energy is a beautiful thing! High frequency foods are our bodies' most powerful healers, while processed foods are their most powerful destroyers; whether food will build your health or break it down depends entirely on how you use it. Getting your food intake right has the power to transform your reality, the way you see yourself, and your notions of what is and isn't possible.

From the outside in, it's hard to imagine just how much becomes available from this one single choice. This is why it usually takes a wake-up call to set us down this path. In my case, a diagnosis of skin cancer was the powerful catalyst that first inspired me to change the way I ate; and as I did, I began seeing life in new ways. This was not something I had to *try* to do; it was an evolution of perception that unfolded naturally.

I had arrived at my early thirties with all the markings of outward success. Those thick, wool blankets I had carried on my back for years were not gone, but you could say they were folded up neatly and stored deep under the surface of my mind and heart. I was living in Los Angeles and working in the stressful world of commercial real estate finance. Managing the expectations of others was a balancing act, to say the least. I often worked long hours, was tethered to my Blackberry (yes, I had a Blackberry), and did not have great personal boundaries. Food was still the bane of my existence. And now there was a heaping mound of stress to go along with it. I was managing to keep all the plates spinning in the air, but one trip to the doctor to look at a spot on my nose changed everything.

I now know

that if we are feeling horrible, that is information and it is important to listen to it.

I'll never forget the moment the words fell from her mouth: c-a-n-c-e-r. Two weeks later, I left her office with a large fresh wound down the center of my nose held together with sutures. Ring the bell! This was my wake up call. In addition to being sick all of the time, having no energy, and feeling like crap, my body was speaking to me at a whole new level. I now know that if we are feeling horrible, that is information and it is important to listen to it. My body finally had my undivided attention and I was committed to taking better care of it. I pressed my doctor for preventative measures I could take to better support my health and keep something like this from manifesting again. Unfortunately I came up empty, not because the doc wasn't willing to help me; but because she, like almost all allopathic doctors, was trained only in disease management and knew no more than I did about nutrition and creating overall health.

So, after hitting this roadblock, I began researching foods and other natural remedies to soothe the ailments I was dealing with. I started eating whole foods, emptied out my freezer of all its frozen dinners and snacks, and began taking a few key supplements. The beginning stage of making these changes was both exciting and uncomfortable. Here is the real deal: I had embarrassing gas, a rumbly tummy, extremely smelly armpits to the point that I had to get rid of all my shirts, and worse skin break outs than when I was a kid. You can imagine how much fun that was!

Even though I felt terrible, I felt equally hopeful. Living with those symptoms was no picnic; but I knew deep down inside that all of the toxic junk in my body was making its way out. It had finally been given permission and the environment it needed to do so. There were days I wanted to give up and days I felt extremely inspired. It turns out when you change your diet, your body goes through its own adjustment process. When the body starts getting what it needs, it actually starts detoxifying and working better. And when we stop applying Band-Aids that only conceal imbalances, the body is free to heal and excrete any emotional, mental, and physical toxins it's been holding onto.

Since the real cause of disease is often rooted in our mental, emotional, and spiritual planes, it is not only the body that needs to release toxins. Negative thoughts and feelings, and past traumatic events, actually create excess amounts of acid in the body that it cannot assimilate. The body needs to allow these thoughts, feelings, and events to rise to the surface to be expressed and released for true healing to occur. To go a step further down the energetic rabbit hole to the quantum truth of this phenomenon, the atoms that make up the cells of your body are mostly empty space. The empty space between the nucleus, and the electrons circling around the nucleus, is where negative energy can become stuck. When the atoms in our bodies become dense with this negative energy, the electrons whirl at a slower rate and we begin to resonate more with a lower vibrational frequency. The good news is, that if given half a chance, the body will naturally try to clear negative energy and release toxins. As it does, there is less density and more light as faster-moving energy within the atom causes the electrons to whirl faster and faster, thereby raising your vibrational frequency.

When the atoms in our bodies become dense with this negative energy, the electrons whirl at a slower rate and we begin to resonate more with a lower vibrational frequency.

Think of a long-term smoker. When they are still smoking, they may have only a small hack, but when they quit they will start coughing deeply all of the time. Once the exterior assault has ended, the body is actually able to start clearing out the damage and repairing in the absence of daily abuse. I bow at the feet of the human body. If given half a chance and even a little support, it becomes a healing machine, and I started to experience this miracle firsthand. I began to have more energy. The detoxification became easier. I figured out what worked and what didn't. I learned how to make this process as easy as it could be and discovered how good it felt to feel good! But the thing I never expected when I started to heal my body is how that healing would affect the way I thought, felt, and experienced life—and how much more of my own inner truth it would give me access to.

Inspired Action

- Your body needs your love, consideration, and care. Today, take a moment to nourish your body in one small way.

Inspired action—meaning actions that are infused with the energy of your positive, loving intentions—shifts your energy, lightens your body, and opens you up to new possibilities, even in the smallest doses.

Self-Awareness Saves the Day

Reconnecting to our inner truth is simply a matter of giving ourselves permission to tap back into the intuition and imagination that flowed so naturally when we were children. Self-awareness is the access point to the moment-by-moment discovery of this truth. Awareness is like a built-in force field that, when activated, can save us from pointless and painful detours—and it's always giving us signals, which we either listen to or do not. We have to be tuned to that inner voice that excitedly shouts, "Yes!" when we run across something that piques our interest, and be receptive when it sometimes cautions, "Don't park here, I feel scared" or, "I need some more time to think before making that decision."

When we drown out our internal voice in favor of upholding the status quo, how can we expect to hear the subtler clues that lead us out of harm's way and into greater opportunity and adventure? The answer is, we can't. If we are going to live our truth, we have to wake up, snap out of it, and be willing in every moment to seek a deeper level of self-awareness. It is the only way we'll feel comfortable marching to the beat of our own drummer instead of being led mindlessly around someone else's block.

After years of working closely enough with people to observe the inner workings of human nature, I have come to realize that self-awareness really is the secret sauce to success. The cornerstone of my work lies in helping people to expand their awareness of all aspects of self because the quicker we can become present to our truth and communicate it, the faster we move into a state of energetic flow, making life a whole lot easier.

I know. It takes a great degree of courage to see what you so desperately want to run from; but running from it sucks. It's exhausting, and ultimately futile—because you're never going to outrun your truth. Whether your soul is calling you to clean up your diet, leave a relationship, change jobs, or relocate, having the courage to acknowledge this truth and move toward it rather than away will bring you closer to fulfilling your deepest desires. If reading that last sentence makes you so uncomfortable that you want to toss this book into the fire, know that this is a completely natural response. But even if it feels scary and every instinct might be urging you to turn away, this emerging truth is actually a sign that your soul is calling you in a new and ultimately fabulous direction. The discomfort is an indication that the truth is—as the old saying goes—about to set you free. It doesn't mean you need to change everything overnight and throw your life into a tailspin. Simply start by taking baby steps in the direction of the whisper, honoring it, and continue summoning the courage to keep putting one foot in front of the other.

Inspired Action

- What is one thing you could shift today/this week in order to honor or express more of your truth?

- Do you need to call someone and share your feelings?

- Is it time to tell your boss you feel you deserve a raise?

- Do you need to get support with your health goals?

- Or share a deeply held secret with your partner?

It Feels Like Falling

It is normal and natural to feel uncomfortable when we allow ourselves to finally admit what needs to change. It is something that needs to be felt fully so that the resistance can be cleared from the body and mind. There is an inherent fear that lives within all human beings about falling. Even the mere prospect of making a change can trigger it. Some people have nightmares about actually falling from high places; but it's the metaphorical fears of falling that impact us all daily: the fear of failure, fear of losing our socioeconomic position, fear of being alone, fear of not being able to control how others see us, and fear of our persona not being what we want it to be. After all, we all want to look like we "have it together." However it shows up, the fear of falling is really a fear of falling out of graces with anything with which we have become personally identified. If we indulge it, this fear has the power to suck the energy out of our lives and stop us dead in our tracks.

The fear of falling exists only at the level of the ego and the persona. Soul callings powerfully trigger this fear because their very purpose is to stretch you beyond who you think you are and bring you right to the threshold of your deepest truths. The voice of the soul often flies in the face of all that you have carefully constructed your life to be. You might even feel like you are going a little crazy when your soul first comes to call, because you can sense that it's leading you away from skimming the surface of your life and into much deeper waters. And this is going to require you to embrace change on many levels. Change is a tough one; so much so, that you'll often go to great lengths to organize your life to safeguard against every possibility of major change. But you will only evolve by learning how to dance with what I call "The Dirty C Word." The more you accept this inevitable fact of life and cooperate with it, the more gracefully you will move through changes.

The fear of falling can feel like facing a mini death—whether it's the death of the way you used to do things, what you used to be interested in, or what you believed to be important.

The fear of falling can feel like facing a mini death—whether it's the death of the way you used to do things, what you used to be interested in, or what you believed to be important. It can help us if we remember that the old must get washed away to reveal the new. We cannot receive and support the higher frequency of our soul until we release old energy. We may want to raise our frequency, but in truth our normal state of being is high frequency. It is only the thoughts, feelings, beliefs, toxins, and patterns that are keeping our frequency low. Release those and you will rise. The tough part about releasing is that we are often called to do so before the new opportunity shows up. For example, imagine that you are in a relationship in which you have felt disconnected and unhappy for many years.

Up until this point, you've stayed because you don't know anything different and you've become accustomed to your current lifestyle. Maybe you are afraid of falling in some of the ways listed above.

But what if you caught a glimpse of the larger possibility that exists on the other side of your discontent? What if you found out that when this relationship is over, you would meet a new partner that you feel deeply and soulfully connected to? What if you knew that the reward of telling the truth and allowing an unsatisfying situation to be released from your experience will be having a partner who understands your evolution, honors it, and enhances it? If you could see the destination that your current unhappiness is ultimately calling you toward, wouldn't it be easier to leave the disconnected partnership? Of course it would, because you would be excited about the reality that is in the process of becoming, rather than lamenting the reality that currently *is*.

For better or for worse, life continually calls us to take these leaps of faith.

However, we don't always see all of the possibilities that lie ahead. For better or for worse, life continually calls us to take these leaps of faith. And there can be no growth or expansion without developing unwavering faith in this never-ending process of becoming. Seriously, to do anything great, your faith will be tested to the point where you almost lose it; but moving forward in the presence of doubt is how real faith is developed. Only by testing and trusting our own intuition will we find the willingness to move in the direction of our soul's calling in the absence of tangible evidence to support it.

When you have developed faith in yourself to the point of acting on it, what happens next is a rising up of experiences that will show you beyond a shadow of a doubt that your faith was perfectly placed. This confirmation then becomes the fuel for taking the next, and even bigger, steps that will follow. As this cycle continues, and more trust is built and then supported, eventually you start to see the grand design in all of it. More is revealed as we continue to step through our fear, listen to our intuition, and have unwavering faith in the universe and ourselves.

It may be difficult to see it when transformation is underway, but something new is always in the process of being born when something old is fading away. In times of change, we tend to focus the bulk of our energy on what is coming apart, while losing sight of what is in the process of being created. It is our creative energy, our commitment to forward thinking, and our belief in the process that continually propel us forward toward that which is calling our name. Sometimes the truth can cut like a knife at the first realization; but in the end we realize this breaking apart was necessary in order to discover the seeds of true freedom. Whatever is awakening inside of you, however faint, know that it wants to be heard and cultivated, and that it is safe to do so.

> **Whatever is awakening inside of you,** however faint, know that it wants to be heard and cultivated, and that it is safe to do so.

The way I have come to see it is, at some point, each of us has to decide how we are going to live this life. Will we dedicate this lifetime to appearances? To the collection of expensive stuff? To an ongoing campaign to get people to approve of or admire us? Or, will we dedicate this unique experience to fully expressing all that we are inside and all that we have come forth to create?

The choice is yours. You have been given this life to live; and to live it powerfully, you must be courageous, vulnerable, open, and truthful. Once you have reconnected to the truth of what your soul is seeking to express in this lifetime, you have only to release that which stands in the way of its unfolding. It doesn't happen overnight, and in fact, like the birth process itself, there are layers of resistance that need to be honored and softened; but I promise, this is an unfolding that is not to be missed.

The next section of this book will support you in fanning the spark that has been lit within your soul. It will show you how to create the space the spark needs in order to grow into a beautiful flame. It will guide you to RELEASE anything that stands in the way of you expressing your most authentic truth. But before you can begin releasing, you first need to locate any old energy that is manifesting in you as poor health, excess weight, discontent, lack, limitation, or fear. The following are a series of exercises designed to help you get to your truth. Curl up on the couch with a cup a tea and a journal, and start opening the door to your soul. Invite it in like an old, beloved friend, and allow it to speak through you. Listen to what comes up and write it down. Cry if you need to, laugh if you want to, and get angry if you must about the years your voice has gone unheard. But please remember where this process is leading you: to fly your truth flag loud, proud, and without apology.

Inspired Action:
Reflections on Truth

This exercise will support you in taking small steps in the direction of your truth. Find a favorite journal and some time to ponder these questions, then write down your responses:

- Where in my life do I experience the fear of falling?
- What am I most fearful of?
- How have I constructed my life in order to avoid feeling that fear?
- How have I held myself back in life because of fear?
- What am I feeling called to do, be, experience, or explore in my life?

Asking yourself these questions takes courage. It is much easier to sit on the couch and watch a sitcom than to do the deep inner work that creates massively awesome transformation. You don't need to do anything with your answers for now except gently acknowledge their truth and give them permission to be. Truth has a powerful way of changing our lives. Just acknowledging it is enough to spark new energy. Trust that this exercise in truth carries the seeds that will flourish into a beautifully awakened life. And, if these questions are helpful and you are ready to go deeper, you can refer to the back of the book to the section entitled *Introspection*.

SECTION II

Release

Release

Once we have identified the ways that we keep the lid on to avoid acknowledging our deeper truth, the next phase of the transformational process is to begin gently taking that lid off. This requires us to become aware of fun stuff like painful emotions, limiting conclusions, and negative mindsets that are still operating under the surface of our consciousness so that we can finally release them. In the beginning of this phase in the transformation process, many people begin to feel uncomfortable—both with resisting the status quo and with what they intuitively sense wants to be created in its place. There is a faint feeling that some aspects of your life are no longer fitting like a glove—like the caterpillar right before it emerges as the butterfly, it must wiggle and squirm to set itself free from the cocoon. As the release of the old and the birth of something new continues, it's typical to feel lost in a life that used to feel so familiar, a sense of free-falling, or like a part of the old "you" is dying. This process may bring up emotions within you that range from uncomfortable to terrifying.

Now, before you run for the hills thinking *Who in their right mind would ever want to experience these feelings?,* stick with me. This phase is a clearing for accessing the greatest joy and most fulfilling experiences of your lifetime.

As the release of the old and the birth of something new continues, it's typical to feel lost in a life that used to feel so familiar, a sense of free-falling, or like a part of the old "you" is dying.

Before we start releasing, let's dive back down the quantum rabbit hole to understand what is going on at the energetic level. The human body is made up of protons, electrons, and neutrons. The protons and neutrons that hold the bulk of our mass are made of a trio of particles called quarks (possibly my favorite word ever!). Quarks don't take up much room and they make up only a tiny percentage of the proton and neutron mass. Gluons that hold the quarks together have no mass. So basically, the atoms of the body are almost entirely empty space. But is space really empty? Heck no, there are wave functions and invisible quantum fields—there is a ton of information in the space, and frequencies associated with that information. Release is a process of releasing the low frequency emotions, thought patterns, and information found in the "empty" spaces of your body, along with anything in the physical realm that is not supporting the positive growth and expansion in your life.

NBD....No big deal at all, right?!

In all seriousness, it is a very big deal and we need to complete this step so that we are free to create something new: a lighter and more radiant version of ourselves. When we take the lid off by stopping addictive behaviors tied to food, drink, checking out, compulsions, and complacency, we begin to clear our way to health. In the same way a patch of soil must be cleared of weeds to make way for new seeds to sprout, we must release the energy from our past in order to allow our soul frequency to emerge. Put simply, this is a time to till the soil of your consciousness in order to free it from hindrances, so that it can support and sustain your awesomeness.

Before I get into exactly what this transformational phase entails, I want to distinguish that the process of releasing is distinct from the concept of "letting go." If you've ever confided in a friend about a problem you were having, only to have her reply with a casual, "Just let it go," you have already experienced how annoying this can be. The expectation is to just *stop* feeling how you feel, and typically it only makes you want to dig your heels in further and take no action.

There's a reason why we hold on to things even when they are no longer working. There's a reason why we grasp for a sense of stability, for a feeling of control over our lives and a guarantee about what the future holds. But trying to "just let go" of what the ego is fiercely clinging onto sets up a tug-of-war inside of us that keeps us stuck in the very situations we are seeking freedom from. On the contrary, releasing is a process. The idea of "releasing" what we've outgrown is like a gentle setting down of an old way of being, in favor of a way that is more fluid and effective. It's an opening to the reality that is waiting for us on the other side. There's a calm, a peacefulness, and a sense of flow when our intention is to release from—rather than let go of—the yucky stuff.

> Only by unpacking the pain
> we tried not to feel in the past can we free ourselves from the control that pain has over us in the present.

It's also important to note that releasing is not simply about painting a shiny layer over painful thoughts and feelings, or minimizing them with trite memes painted over a sunset like "Just be positive." It is not an eagle flying through the sky with "let your wings soar." It doesn't do any good to try and smile over the top of misery. Releasing is finding the courage and the willingness to look within the deepest caverns of your truth in order to uncover negative thought patterns and blocked emotions that you've been carrying for years—or even eons—so you can finally allow yourself to feel them and heal them. Only by unpacking the pain we tried not to feel in the past can we free ourselves from the control that pain has over us in the present. The process of release gives us the freedom and space to acknowledge our deeper truth and live our soul's purpose.

Releasing is like a trust fall into the unknown that causes us to call into question the very identities that we've constructed our lives around. You may start to challenge what were previously foregone conclusions about your life and yourself; conclusions such as, "*This is the type of person I am. This is what I do for a living. This is the body weight and the level of energy that I have. These are the commitments and values I guide my life by.*" If you think you are an extrovert, super social, and a great administrative assistant who secretly wishes you could lose twenty pounds, you may come out of the other side of releasing to find that you are an introvert who loves yoga, wants to own her own business, and truly loves herself fully. Stranger things have happened and trust me, releasing the old is a powerful step in starting to live your truth.

The awareness that the persona you've constructed is actually standing in the way of your authentic self-expression can trigger some intense feelings. You may feel like you are no longer a part of the agreed-upon reality you have existed in for your entire life. There is deep emotion being purged at this time; emotions that you may have denied or repressed from much earlier in your lifetime. It is a time of introspection and contemplation, reconciling the past, and discovering who you desire to be and what you desire to experience in the future. Release brings everything previously hidden up for evaluation. We start to ask ourselves *why* we have chosen the things we have chosen and whether they are still serving us.

The Myth Of The "Perfect" Life

For most of my life, my identity was closely tied up with my image of myself as a "career girl." I worked in a high-paced and high-stress industry, and invested most of my energy toward meeting my goal of creating professional and financial success. I had had a few relationships throughout my 20s and early 30s, and had always dreamed of being married and having kids; but I felt afraid of this level of commitment. It all seemed so "big girl." Funny that working in a difficult industry in a high rise building in L.A. didn't seem as "big girl" as the prospect of marriage and babies.

The truth is, romantic relationships always scared me. I lived with a deep fear of getting divorced and reliving what my parents had gone through. You see, until you go through the transformational, alchemical process I'm taking you through now, all that is really available is fearing something that you have seen others live. This typically manifests either as trying desperately to do the opposite of what you witnessed, or unconsciously falling into line with the examples laid out before. The fear of divorce was almost a part of my DNA, and it kept me closed off to love in many ways. I just didn't feel safe a lot of the time and did not allow myself to connect with my heart to many people–especially those whom I felt had the ability to break it and run.

And then, I met Travis. When I met my love, that hardened shell began to melt away. He was like kryptonite for the emotional walls I had worked so hard to build. For the first time, I was willing to acknowledge my fear of intimacy and lean in anyway. For some reason he didn't scare me like others had; instead, he intrigued me. I was willing to risk the potential of heartbreak for the experience of spending my moments with him in person or talking for hours on the phone each night. From the very beginning, I felt like there were forces much bigger than either of us, drawing us together for reasons I came to understand years later.

From the very beginning,

I felt like there were forces much bigger than either of us, drawing us together for reasons I came to understand years later.

Travis was like a modern day knight in shining armor: six feet tall with a lean build, a big smile, and a kindness about him that I had never before experienced in a man. He was quiet on the outside, passionate on the inside; and the moment this creative and intuitive man walked into my life, everything inside of me said *yes*: *put both feet into this and allow it to flourish.*

Was there fear? For shizzle! A lot of it! But love won every time and I moved through it. At every new step of our coming together (exclusively dating, going on our first vacation, and meeting each other's families) we kept moving closer to the call that we both felt. Within two weeks of meeting each other we both knew we were in love, and a year later we were engaged.

It was, up until that point, the happiest time of my life. Travis felt like home. He loved me in a way I had never been loved: patiently, attentively, and quietly. Meeting Travis was like a fairytale, and like in every good fairytale, I imagined us riding off into the sunset together, living the perfect life. For the first year of our marriage, this is exactly what unfolded.

Both Travis and I grew up in small beach towns in Southern California; but that is where the outward similarities of our childhoods ended. His parents had been married for almost forty years and had built an extremely successful business together that employed many of the family members, including Travis. Everyone seemed to be very close. As a product of divorce, this seemed like a slice of perfect family heaven to me. It was something I had always hoped I would one day experience.

When I say it was a bit of a fairytale, it really was. The person I used to be wanted all things big, grand, and exciting; and the celebration of our union certainly followed suit. Our wedding took place at an exclusive resort in Santa Barbara. We were married in the evening in a circular ballroom adorned with candles and flowers, and we danced the night away with one of the biggest '80s cover bands in CA. When Travis and I combined our lives, almost everything expanded exponentially. We had more material things, more money, more friends, and busier schedules than either of us had ever experienced individually. We could now afford a completely new lifestyle filled with all kinds of goodies. It felt free and fun and we made the most of everything.

Everyone has dreams and fantasies of the life we think we someday want to live; but often we don't realize what is driving our desire for those dreams.

Everyone has dreams and fantasies of the life we think we someday want to live; but often we don't realize what is driving those dreams. We think they originate from the purest place, but oftentimes they do not. Most of the time, they are based on images spoon-fed to us by the media. From the time we are children, we are steeped in information about what the "perfect" life should look like, and many of us never look up from the roadmap we were handed to see if we really want to visit the destination.

During the Release phase, you may find yourself stopping to ask: is the life I am aspiring towards really perfect for me? I will help you answer that right now. Many times, the answer is no. So often, I see people chasing things like the bigger house, the more prestigious career, the new car, the better body, or the next lavish vacation, only to arrive at what they thought would make them happy and discover that it doesn't.

I refer to this phenomenon lovingly as the mid-life wakeup call, although for those who I describe as "old souls," the alarm may go off as early as their 20s or 30s. Whenever or however this wakeup call occurs, it brings with it the realization that chasing after material things or status in hopes of finding inner happiness is a dead-end road. My advice? Turn back now before you drive off into the dirt! I don't say this to burst your bubble. I say this because we often think some *thing* is going to fix or fill the emptiness inside, and it never, ever does.

To quit wasting our precious time and energy chasing external trinkets, we must start looking within. We have to release the fantasy of the "perfect" life in order to arrive at a new reality and start to live a truly healthy life. Because nothing fuels addiction like working hard towards a vision of perfection only to realize when you get there that it doesn't fit, and to then feel too trapped and powerless to do anything about it. Trust me on this one.

The life Travis and I envisioned ourselves living was to be the perfect picture of stability. We would never have a care in the world financially. We would live down the way from his family, and not far from mine. I would be in the PTA and he would coach the kids in sports. We would celebrate our birthdays at the same restaurant in the same booth. It all looked good on paper, but unbeknownst to us, we were slowly morphing into a Stepford-type existence.

You remember it, right?

Duty valued over happiness, stress more common than peace, and using your mind considered far superior to listening to your heart.

Part of this transformation was due to the two of us striving to conform to the ideals of others, and part of it was our own internal pressures to show up in a certain way. Along with the fairytale state we lived in during our first year of marriage, we slowly started to buy into those subtle overtones that seemed to be simply a part of adulthood. I was unknowingly beginning to replicate a familiar environment. One of duty being valued over happiness, stress more common than peace, and using your mind considered far superior to listening to your heart.

These unspoken rules dictate the lives of so many people, and most of the time the people have no idea the rules even exist. A series of events occurs that causes us pain, trauma, or sadness; and the decisions we make as a result of those events create an inauthentic way of being in the world. As we seek safety and comfort in any number of ways, we slowly become distanced from the depths of who we are and instead begin to emulate the frequency of those around us. Caught up in appearances, fun events, being social, and trying to create "perfect" all over our lives, we wash over the soul's call and ignore the whisper that is always there waiting for us to hear it.

Trying to Tune Out Evolution

After we had been married for a little over a year, Travis and I started talking about having a child. We both felt nervous about the prospect. We each had very different reasons, but the fear was nonetheless real. By this point, my physical healing was coming along very well and I was confident that my body was ready to grow a healthy baby. Even through all of the fear, I felt a knock at my door that it was time.

I have known and worked with many women who intuitively felt when a baby was ready to come into their lives long before it happened, and this was my experience as well. I knew that even if I felt unready, this baby was ready. When it is time to evolve, there always comes a gentle knock on the door. It may be a child, like it was for me, but it can also be a new career, a health scare, a new love, or a change in residence. It can be anything, really. It is a yearning for that next step. If you have never felt this, I can only say that you will know it when you do; and that possibly even by reading this book, you will begin to hear the subtle whispers that have always been there.

The resistant person will know they need to change something, anything, or everything; and yet they will still dig their heels in and do everything they can to turn the other way.

Many of us are unconsciously trying to put the brakes on our evolution around every corner we go. Two of the king-pin strategies that we use are resistance and perfectionism. These are both ways that we unconsciously try to control our evolution and stop forward motion. Some people are very resistant to almost everything; these are the folks who, when you ask them if they want to do something new, say 'no' right off the bat. If you give your opinion, they have a contradictory opinion—or two or three.

They're resisting life, meaning they are using their energy to push away unwanted experiences or to avoid change, rather than focusing their energy on the creation of what they *do* want.

For example, a resistant person doesn't want to go to the doctor when they are sick. They will get mad when you keep asking and they will give you many reasons why they don't need to go. That's resistance. That's stopping evolution, along with halting any sort of healing. The resistant person will know they need to change something, anything, or everything; and yet they will still dig their heels in and do everything they can to turn the other way.

A true perfectionist

will turn the other way when her husband is cheating, exercise when her foot hurts, not sleep the night before a party, and engage in a host of other unhealthy behaviors to uphold the image.

The other side of this spectrum is perfectionism—aww, my BFF for so many years! Although on the surface it presents differently from resistance, perfectionism is just another form of seeking control. We decide that we are going to look perfect, be perfect, have the perfect job, and live the perfect life; and we need that perfectionism so much that we would sacrifice almost anything in order to avoid being a misfit in our picture of what life is supposed to look like. A true perfectionist will turn the other way when her husband is cheating, exercise when her foot hurts, not sleep the night before a party, and engage in a host of other unhealthy behaviors to uphold the image. A perfectionist will say, "Of course, life is not perfect. Everyone knows that," because most perfectionists are not present to their ways and how they affect their life and the people around them.

The real down and dirty truth is that life is messy. If you look over any one person's lifetime, there are so many events that have happened. No one leaves the human experience unscathed. When we're in perfectionism, we're trying to fit into an ideal that doesn't exist in an attempt to control our evolution. This hinders each person from accessing deeper levels of trust and love and from surrendering to the whispers of their soul. Some degree of resistance or perfectionism is present in most people's lives—often in spades. You can't stop evolution—not even Wonder Woman can, because trying to do so goes against Mother Nature. It is fruitless and a waste of energy because the Mother of all Mothers always wins. If it is your time to hear your soul's whisper, you will have to almost destroy yourself to try and drown it out; and in the end, you won't.

Again, all of this comes down to fear and resistance to change. But when we try to stand in the way of the inevitable, dis-ease and addictions are given a fertile ground in which to grow and the energy is drained out of us. Have you ever been around someone who looks dull in the eyes?

Like the lights are on, but no one is home? They have no vibrancy, energy, or excitement for life, and they seem like they're living a very rote existence.

We did not come here to wither; we came here to grow and inspire and be our most radiant selves. The human life is to be lived fully. It is the only way that our eyes will sparkle. When evolution comes knocking, as it will for everyone, the path of least resistance in the long run is to *listen*.

Inspired Action

- In what areas of your life are you striving for perfection?

- Where are you in resistance to what is currently present in your life, or trying to control the natural unfolding of events?

- By becoming aware of these patterns, you create space for them to change.

The Dirty C Word

No one likes change; really, no one. We are not wired for it and we almost never accept it gracefully—unless of course the change is that you just won the lottery, or something miraculous happens in your life and everything lines up in a way that doesn't require you to have to stretch or expand. When other, less cushy changes come knocking on your door, they are always an invitation to grow. You may not consciously be choosing it, but your soul is inviting it in. The soul knows what you are meant to do and it is always showing you the way, even when you are not listening, and even when you allow false limitations and beliefs to hold you back. It is similar to the GPS system in your car. If you fail to get over in time to get off at the correct exit, it will redirect you to the next exit and give you a new route. It just takes much longer than it needs to if we refuse to listen.

A year into Travis's and my marriage, our GPS was sending us signals to take the next exit off the current road we were traveling on. There was a discontent in both of us that was palpable. The discontent was not so much with each other as much as it was with the life we had constructed around us. We had hit the mid-marker of our lives, and this pivotal point was a time of reflection. It suddenly hit us that life is short, and so naturally we began to assess how we were spending our time and where our choices were leading us.

For Travis and me, the prospect of spending time in the same way for another several decades was sad—living in the same house for thirty years, working at jobs that were not in alignment with our souls, and defining ourselves by how well we acquired things. The realization of where we were headed was heavy for both of us. The chasm between how things looked on the outside and how they felt on the inside was growing wider to the point of becoming intolerable. We wanted to dance to a different beat, listen to a new rhythm, and change the feeling of vacancy to a sense of purpose.

Sometimes in life we need a little nudge to see the truth. To be more accurate, we often need a good shove out of our comfort zone to change. It was hard for Travis and me to see what was so close in front of us, but our souls sent us the perfect messenger for change: the birth of a beautiful baby boy.

To say that our son changed our lives would be a massive understatement. The time and circumstances under which Jameson chose to arrive on planet Earth triggered a series of changes that are far beyond what many couples experience when a child is born. His energy moved *fast*. I became pregnant quickly, and it was as if he came in on a lightning bolt; he began to shake things up from the time he was in my belly. Jameson's energy was very strong. I knew at a fundamental, deep, inner-compass level that the experience of becoming his mom was going to change my life in ways I couldn't begin to predict. The changes started happening even before he was born.

LOVE + TRUTH

My soul's whispers came fast during pregnancy, as if someone had flicked on a switch. I suddenly found myself in the fast lane on the highway of super consciousness. It began with the repetitive thoughts about the words "love" and "truth." At the time, I was not sure why LOVE belonged with TRUTH or why they came in that order. It wasn't truth and love, it was specifically LOVE + TRUTH. The words appeared in my consciousness as a visual that was very specific in all of its randomness.

One day, upstairs in my office, I decided to type these two words into Google and pushed enter. I didn't know it at the time, but this would come to open up a door to a flood of new knowledge that was actually old knowledge I was about to remember (stick with me here; you will get it!). I selected the website in the search query that I was immediately drawn to. The page had tons of written content and there were number sequences such as 1110004443332222, and color sequences such as magenta-gold-white-violet, that appeared together in a certain repetitive order.

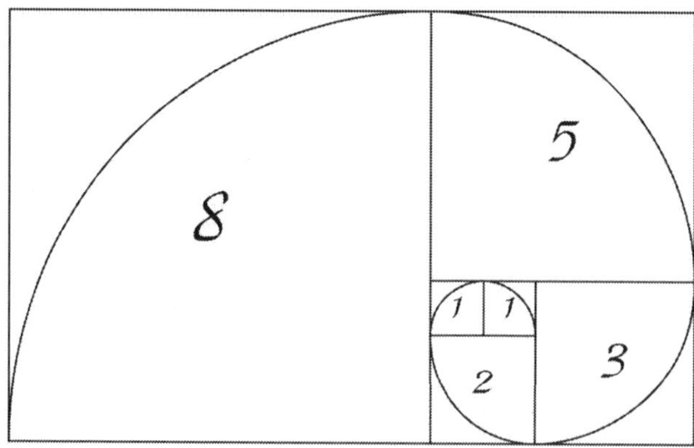

The repetition of these sequences was fascinating to me and it spoke to me enough that I researched it further and eventually found myself discovering a famous number sequence that has fascinated mathematicians, artists, designers, and scientists for centuries. It is known as the Golden Ratio or The Fibonacci Sequence. The Golden Ratio describes the rate at which exponential growth happens both in nature as a whole as well as in our bodies. Here is the number sequence:

1 + 1= 2

1 + 2 = 3

2 + 3 = 5

3 + 5 = 8

5 + 8 = 13

And so on. The sequence 1, 1, 2, 3, 5, 8, 13, 21, 34, 55, 89, 144, 233, 377, 610, 987 ... also depicts what is known as the Fibonacci curve which is most often illustrated in the cross section of a nautilus shell.

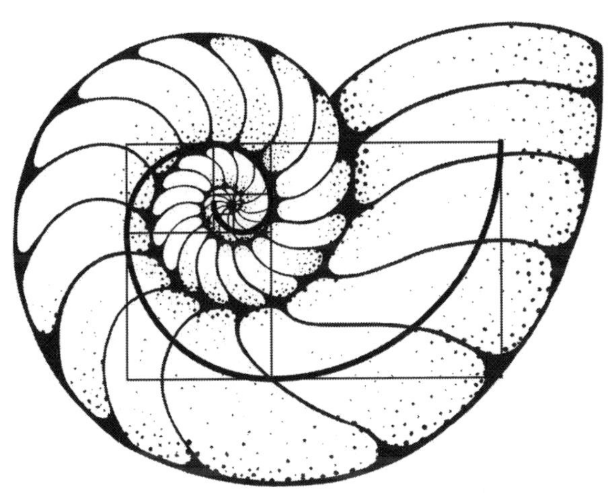

It depicts the pattern of growth in all living things. The number of petals in a flower consistently follows the Fibonacci sequence. Famous examples include the lily, which has three petals; buttercups, which have five; the chicory, which has twenty-one; and the daisy, thirty-four. The DNA molecule measures thirty-four angstroms long by twenty-one angstroms wide for each full cycle of its double helix spiral. Galaxies, hurricanes, shells, the flight patterns of animals, the development of the human face, da Vinci's paintings, and the way tree branches form and split, all follow the Fibonacci sequence.

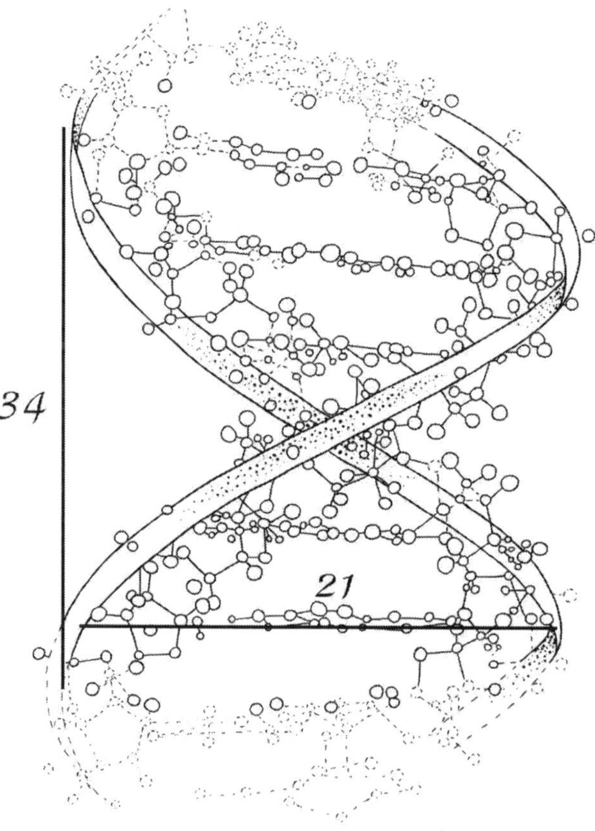

I hate math and yet, I was fascinated by this built-in numbering system of the cosmos. This is the thread of evolution that ties nature and all living things together with the stars and galaxies. There is more to this thing called life than we can even begin to realize when viewing it from a purely superficial level. We are profoundly designed miracles and the two words LOVE + TRUTH led me down the road to discovering this expanded view of life and myself. This is not some strange sci-fi movie, although I felt like I was in one as I read through pages and pages of text and codes and went deeper down the rabbit hole of ancient science and math.

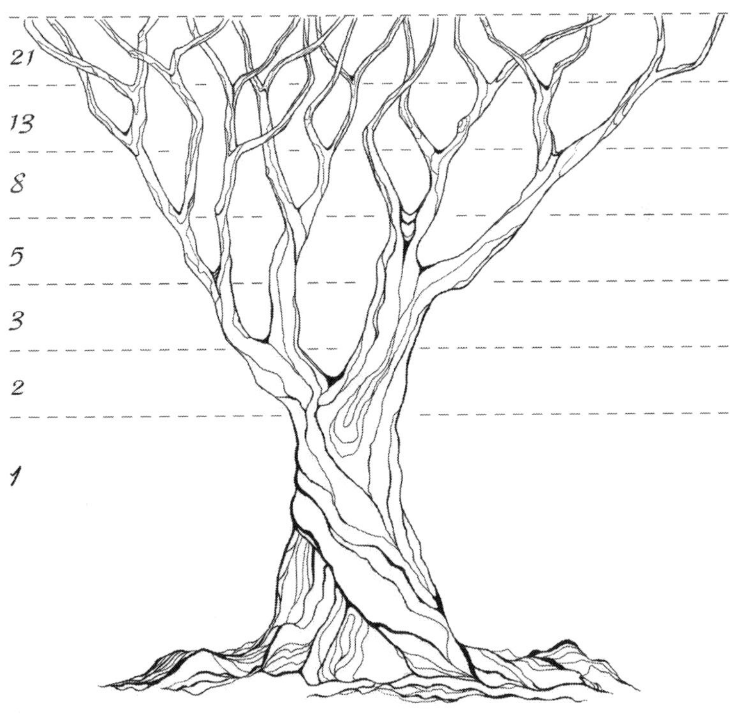

I had a little laugh to myself, because who would have thought that the girl who got a C in high school geometry would care about this stuff; and yet, I couldn't seem to stop reading. Although my mind was blown, these sequences somehow felt as familiar as my own face. This would prove to be the first pivotal stop along a cosmic scavenger hunt for information that spoke directly to my soul. Unbeknownst to me, I was gathering information and wisdom as I followed the guidance of those whispers. This was not Star Trek, but I was definitely being beamed up to a new level of consciousness in my life. This expansion of myself continued through my pregnancy and escalated much more rapidly after our son's birth. Travis and I were changing, growing, and expanding at an entirely new rate of speed, and Jameson was the catalyst for our rapid-fire evolution.

Although my mind was blown,
these sequences somehow felt as familiar as my own face.

Everything happens in its right time without mistake; but instead of surrendering to the divine order, we often waste much of our precious time wishing things happened sooner, later, or never happened at all. In using our energy to resist all that is happening, we are too busy to stop and listen to the whispers until they become screams.

We tax our internal GPS, strain our physical bodies, and stress ourselves out... and for what? To spend my energy questioning why these codes had popped onto the movie screen at this particular time in my life, or to judge myself for thinking about the concept of LOVE + TRUTH like it was my first crush, was futile. It was just so. It may not have made sense on one hand, but it made perfect sense on the other, because everything in nature happens in divine order.

There is a rhythm and a flow to all things and every component has a specific role to play in the creative process. Animals, unlike humans, respect the timing and flow of nature and move in harmony within the tapestry of life. Do you know how long the beetle species has been on the planet? Only about 300 million years, and I am going to venture a guess that only beings who live in flow with nature can survive for that long. Going against Mother Nature is certain death eventually. It is only in the last short period of time that mankind has begun to move away from nature and to fear the nature of our own wild soul. Over the history of time, empires have fallen whenever humans deviate too far from nature. Mother Nature always wins. She always survives and those who know they are part of Her tend to prevail. Your soul, Mother Nature, and the universe have one amazing thing in common: they are whispering clues to bring you closer to the path that is meant for you. You can heed the call and live who you came here to be, powerfully and courageously, or you can turn on Seinfeld reruns with a bottle of wine and a TV dinner, ignore the whisper and tune out your greatness.

Inspired Action

You are a grand pattern and a sequence of mathematics. When the patterning is interrupted, your health and life go out of balance.

- What feels out of balance in your life?

Slowing down to evaluate what you need is important.

- How can you be creative with your schedule to find more balance and harmony?
- How can you create new systems that give you more freedom and time?

Knowing It

You know how you sometimes KNOW something, even when you don't want to know it? Like when you sense that a boyfriend is cheating on you, or that a sound your car is making really should be checked out; but you try to pretend that you don't know what you know? Travis and I were like that. We sensed that life as we had known it was about to change. During the Release stage, the catalyst will blow open the door to expose the truth and there is nowhere to hide from the new levels of awareness that it exposes.

Within six months of our son's birth, Travis and I began actively working on our relationship to unearth our individual truths and better understand the energy that was rising in each of us. We cried, we got angry, we talked through all hours of the night. We located things in one another that we couldn't see in ourselves; and, in so doing, we began to purge lifetimes of low frequency energy and the effects of the experiences that created it.

It felt like we were lifting out of one reality, hovering over it, and looking down at everything; but we were no longer participating fully in it.

We got used to a new level of conversation in our own household—conversations about awareness and consciousness—and our understanding of our spiritual nature grew as we got more familiar with the soul frequency that was starting to shine through. Speaking our truth to one another was terrifying at first; but over time, we became more comfortable with it, and each time we could accept each other's communication with grace and understanding, our relationship grew stronger.

This was the beginning of a major upshift in the frequency of our lives and our partnership. We were shedding the old and making the space for the new. It felt like we were lifting out of one reality, hovering over it, and looking back observing everything; but we were no longer participating fully in it. A clearing was being created and from this empty space, a whole new way of living would be born.

Inspired Action

- What do you know that you are pretending not to know?

  This may be buried so deep you don't see it, but if you keep asking, something will rise to the surface. It may make you nervous to think about it, and yet, ultimate freedom happens by identifying your truth.

Speaking It

Knowing it and speaking it are two very different things. There is a time of reconciliation and processing between the moment we become conscious of something that needs to change and when we give ourselves permission to speak that change into existence. Words are powerful creators and each time we say something, we give it power. So, it is important that we are solid in our knowingness before we speak.

After months of wading through the water under the bridge of our lives and our marriage, getting really real in conversation with each other and ourselves, Travis and I were ready—or should I say, we were fearfully pushing ourselves forward—to speak our desired changes into the world. This is the point where many people turn back from the process of transformation. This is where they almost want to throw up from feeling sick with fear. This is where one wants to hit the escape hatch or dive into some heavy addictions in order to not feel the intensity while retreating back to the world of perceived safety.

Travis and I both had some powerful truths to speak into existence and they went like this: my husband no longer wanted to live his life by someone else's standards. He realized it wasn't too late to live a life that fulfilled him and that included leaving his family's business and making a career of his longtime passion for music instead. I wanted to find some way to use all of the aspects of myself—from businesswoman to poet, to health enthusiast, to soulfully spiritual moonchild. If the alarm in your head is going off, saying something like this is irresponsible or pipe-dreamy or anything along those lines, you are certainly not alone. When you speak a huge change into existence, there is always going to be backlash, shock, hurt, and a whole lot of overt and covert tactics to get you to back down to living in a way that makes the people around you comfortable. I'll share much more about how to handle this when and if you encounter it in the final section of this book because this is exactly what happened for us.

When you speak a huge change into existence,

there is always going to be backlash, shock, hurt, and a whole lot of overt and covert tactics to get you to back down to living in a way that makes the people around you comfortable.

Over the next few months, we were deep into the dismantling of the life we knew and moving fast into a whole new reality. When you tell the truth, many people in your life will be triggered in some way by the telling. Changing how you eat, behave, live, believe or communicate will cause others to question their own reality, which is an uncomfortable self-inquiry. Turns out, there were some people who supported us, and others that did everything they could to try and stop our evolution, even though we know this is simply not possible.

We moved out of the spacious home we had decorated to our liking, the one we were going to live in for the next thirty years. My husband left his career, we sold half of our furniture, and moved into a tiny rental twenty minutes away. We downsized our life in a matter of days and began to heal from the wounds caused by the resistance that some of those close to us had in response to our change.

I would absolutely love to tell you that we moved on quickly after that and wrap up this story right here with a big red bow; but that is not how things went down. We didn't just move houses, change careers, or find ourselves in discord with some people. Our entire construct of who we were was being dismantled. On the outside it looked like we made a few adjustments to our lifestyle, but on the inside it felt like a fuse had just been detonated and the high-rise building that was our life was blown to pieces in a few short minutes.

I have worked with clients who enter this transformational phase as a result of a major change in one area of their life, and with others whose experience of Release is more like a domino effect where one change triggers the next. The latter was true in our case, and the life-demolition sent us whirling, emotionally and mentally.

The F*** Word

We all have it. We all don't want to have it and we all build our entire realities around trying not to feel it. Good ole fear is at the heart of all of lack, limitation, and every other block that holds us back from our awesomeness. Fear is an alarm system, one that is built in to keep us safe. You need fear if you are standing on the side of a cliff looking over the edge, or if someone is walking up to you in a dark alley, or for a multitude of reasons that warrant you taking precautions to keep yourself safe.

If you let fear control your life,

you will be tending to false alarms when there is no fire and you will exhaust yourself in the process.

Seriously, without the fear alarm in these instances, it would not be a good scenario. But there are many instances where fear keeps us stuck, unable to locate our truth, and move forward in situations where there is no real imminent danger. In these situations, I am a big fan of making fear your friend instead of resisting it, because we all know that what you resist persists. If you can allow fear in and feel it fully, you can dissipate this energy fast by letting it move right through your body. The problem with fear is that "imminent danger" kind of fears and the "keep you stuck in life" kind of fears often ring the same alarm. This alarm can make it confusing to tell whether you are doing something outright dangerous to your wellbeing or whether you are about to make a powerful, though very scary, positive change in your life. Learning to decipher your fear alarm is important. If you let fear control your life, you will be tending to false alarms when there is no fire and you will exhaust yourself in the process.

For the next two years of our lives, Travis and I were answering false alarms as if there was an actual fire. Trying to create a new reality from fear. At the time, I would have told you through the tears that I was being scorched as every single thing we experienced felt like a 3rd degree burn. Over these years, we proceeded to lose all of our savings by making hasty decisions rooted in fear. We ended up having no real income coming into our household and absolutely nothing to show for the money lost. After our inner demolition, it would have been good to stop, wait for the air to clear, and let the dust settle. But instead we exhausted ourselves running from fear, and like most people who have done this eventually realize, it got us nowhere we wanted to go.

Inspired Action

- What would happen if you spoke your deepest darkest truth into existence?

- What are your biggest fears around doing this?

Freedom and energy always surface along with truth. The fear at the beginning is simply part of the journey. The things you see as mistakes or missteps are actually growing you in ways you are yet to see.

Going to Nothing

Don't get too panicked about the words 'going to nothing.' They don't mean that you will walk away from your career, lose all of your money, or instantly exit the only reality that you have ever known. This varsity level transformation was given to Travis and me so we could put words to what many people face during their lives and either feel too shameful to express or cannot find a way to fully describe. I get it because I have lived it, and here is the simple anatomy of what is going on: if you want to build a better life, you need to dismantle everything that doesn't work and build it back even better—meaning, with more integrity than it had before.

Going to nothing is when, post demolition, you are looking out over vacant land in one or more areas of your life before the rebuilding process has begun. When we shed the people, circumstances, and experiences that have been holding us in a reality that no longer supports our soul frequency, what is left in their absence is a lot of empty space. Travis and I had not only lifted off from the reality we knew, like a spaceship leaving earth, we were floating somewhere between earth and the moon; and when we looked through the porthole there was a whole lot of darkness.

At this point, while many of your unconscious blocks and deepest fears begin to be illuminated, it can feel anywhere from uncomfortable to unbearable. It's like some version of Fight Club going on inside of your own brain, between the "you" that you were and the "you" that you are becoming.

It feels like a whole lot of confusion all over the place. The catalyst for this stage of internal struggle, as I have mentioned, can be a trauma such as a loved one dying, a natural disaster, divorce, or losing your job. However, some people initiate this life changing experience for themselves. These people are typically seeking answers to life's deeper questions such as: *What is my purpose? Why am I here? How do I heal? What makes me happy? How can I be more fulfilled? How do I find inner peace?*

Whether it is consciously chosen or appears to come out of the blue, the experience of going to nothing happens in perfect divine order and is a necessary part of Release. You may move through it relatively quickly or it may take time to unfold; but if you can get somewhat comfortable in the space of nothingness, you can rise like a mythical phoenix out of the ashes and shine with power, grace, high virtue, and prosperity in all areas of your life.

After the complete demolition, I felt as though I was slipping through a large slippery tube and picking up speed with no way of stopping myself. One night, I took my son Jameson into his room for bedtime, quietly flicked off the lights, turned on his turtle night-light that projected green stars on the ceiling, took a seat in his grey fabric glider, threw my feet up on the ottoman, and snuggled my boy into my lap. I began gently rocking him, staring down at his sweet face. As soon as he started to drift off to sleep, I began reviewing in my mind all that had unraveled in my life over the past year. I went over and over it in my mind, wondering how things could have worked out differently, how it could have been a smoother path.

I reviewed, in a continuous loop, what I would have liked to say to the people who had been so horribly unsupportive. Mentally, I chastised myself for all the ways that I should have stood up for myself and been stronger, and for all the times I ignored my own inner voice. In that grey chair on that night and every single night for the year leading up to it, I sat there feeling weak, ashamed, broken, and alone in my pain. I wondered if my son would grow up thinking I was a joke. Had I jeopardized his future? I wondered if I had screwed everything up, and it would be a lie to say that I didn't dream of running back to my old life. I wanted out from all of the mess, from all of the devastation. But there was nothing to go back to, nowhere to run.

On this particular night, I got up from the grey glider after reviewing all of the jerks in my life, all of my own faults and blaming everyone who I could think of. I walked two steps over to my son's crib. With tears falling out of my eyes onto his pajamas, I had barely let go of him when my knees buckled and I fell to the floor. I always used to make fun of that kind of stuff in the movies. I thought it was overly dramatic and yet, there I was down on my knees in less than a second or two. Once my knees hit the floor, my chest fell forward as my face hit the carpet and the sobbing became deep and unstoppable. I muffled my cry by burying my face as deep as I could into the pile, and I started calling out to God or really anyone who would listen. And as I rambled on, praying for Him to stop the pain, I was literally shocked and immediately silenced when I heard these five words come through:

"What if you created this?"

I immediately thought to myself, *What, the f***? Why the hell would I create this?* Those five words were like the final dagger in my heart. I was devastated and frustrated screaming in my head, *This is not helping! Why would you say this? How can you do this to me?* At my wits end and in excruciating pain, I already felt abandoned by the person I used to be, cast aside from the only reality I had ever known; and now, God had served up the final blow. Nail the coffin closed. I was torn right open on that floor, sobbing, feeling as though my heart had been smashed into a million pieces.

As I lay in heap on my child's floor, I could barely catch my breath, feeling so completely lost that it would be impossible to find me; and if they did, who the hell was I anyways these days?—I barely recognized myself. The pain was raw, almost paralyzing—and I felt like this very well could be the end for me. Then came nine more words:

"If you created this, than you can un-create this."

It took me a second to process what had just happened. Time stopped and all of a sudden I couldn't feel my body. It was as if someone had slapped me in the face and told me to snap out of it, and then served me up a healthy reminder of my power. I froze. The tears stopped. I knew that this moment mattered. I knew that I had just received something so critically important. The pressure on my heart lifted and I sat up, stunned by what I'd just heard.

Something inside of me had broken free—a massive shift had occurred when I heard those nine little words. I slowly got up off the floor and made my way to the door of my son's room. Something was left on the floor of the bedroom that night. I had died a little again, except this time it wasn't my innocence, trust, and my heart left broken on the floor. It was all of the lids, constructs and beliefs that formed when I was ten years old after my parents' divorce. It was the thirty years of pretending, pleasing, and hiding from the truth that were left on the floor that night.

That night I was transported to the deepest darkest parts of myself only to have them washed clean. I left my son's room that night with a deep knowing of what this meant for my life. Words will never do justice to what I experienced, but I'll give you the cliff notes in an attempt to convey the powerful gift I was given. We create the messiest, most difficult, and painful experiences to call ourselves up to live more authentically. We come here to shake ourselves up, to break ourselves open, and to gasp for air as we breathe in the truth for the first time; and finally we surrender to the fact that we created all of it. We imprison ourselves so that we can break ourselves free and see our true power. Once you know this, life is never the same.

E is For Emotions

Emotions are like the Big Bad Wolf in the eyes of many. I want to write about emotions until the cows come home because expressing them is the key to releasing the old and stepping into the new. Unexpressed emotions are the culprits that keep us stuck in life. We go to such great lengths to avoid feeling our emotions, perhaps because we're afraid that once we allow them to flow we will be incapacitated for months. We fear that once we turn on that faucet, we won't be able to turn it off. But the truth is, when allowed to express freely, the lifespan of an emotion is much like a bell curve: it gathers momentum and intensity until it reaches a crescendo, and then dissipates in intensity as it recedes down the other side.

If we allow this process to occur full force without blocking it, a single feeling will only last sixty to ninety seconds. Doesn't knowing this make the prospect of feeling your feelings so much less daunting? Let's catch our brains up on the facts: if a single emotion lasts sixty seconds, even six different emotional responses will last around six minutes, not six months; and most of us are equipped to handle that. We just have to practice.

It is amazing how much energy adults spend trying *not* to feel. The main emotional difference between children and adults is that children throw their fits openly while adults suppress them, which later manifests in the form of disease. To illustrate how unnatural it is to block our feelings, imagine if everyone was going around trying not to think and being afraid to do so. There would be a whole lot of people walking around looking like aimless robots unable to make a rational decision or carry out a simple task. The exterior world as we know it would come to a screeching halt. Suppressing emotions has the same debilitating effect, except it is the inner world of people that is mostly affected—just as destructive, but more easily hidden.

Up until we reach the age of about two or three years old, we are free emotional beings—and then we are socialized to stop feeling our feelings. For example, if a feeling builds within us and we start up the curve of the bell, often we are met by a parent or teacher who is feeling inconvenienced by our emotion, saying, "Don't cry. Stop it. Go in time-out." When we would have a temper tantrum we may have been told, "Get up off the floor. Don't do that. Stop." But when we stifle our emotions, we never allow them to peak out over the arc of the bell curve and come back down the other side to completion. When this occurs, we become walking storage vessels for unresolved and unexpressed pain. And as we explored in the previous section, this emotional repression often leads to uncontrolled outbursts or numbing out in various ways, and both generally lead to the creation of more pain.

This moment is your opportunity to reconnect fully with your emotional self. This is the time when all bets are off, and you are again free to feel your feelings just as you did when you were a small child, before the world told you not to. That night in Jameson's bedroom, I could no longer pretend to be the victim of all that had happened. I was the co-creator. I had orchestrated something so grand so I could wake up and start living the life that was awaiting me. Being free from the constructs of the past and now profoundly connected to my own inner guidance, took me out of the backseat of the car, put me squarely in the driver's seat, and gave me back the keys to my life.

Inspired Action

- What do you need to cry about?

- Who are you pissed off at?

  Anger is the most repressed emotion in women. It blocks the flow of energy through the body and can keep you stuck in negative patterns.

- What is an action you could take—such as going for a brisk walk or screaming or crying into a pillow—that would give you an opportunity to feel and express your withheld emotions? It takes courage to allow yourself to feel, but it will change your life in the most beautiful ways.

From Victim to Victor

If only he would..., she shouldn't have..., they are holding me back... Thoughts like these are all verbal cues that a victim mentality is running rampant in your field of consciousness. Victimhood is giving over your power to someone else and acting like you don't have a choice in the matter. It is a type of circular reasoning that will keep you on a rat wheel of discontent, chronically complaining, and justifying why things are not going better for you, with no end in sight. Of course, few people walk around consciously thinking that they are victims; and yet, everyone falls prey to this mentality at some point, in some area of their lives, whether they are aware of it or not. Victimhood will strip you of your power the second you give in to its tempting invitation to relinquish responsibility over your life and blame someone or something else for how your life is turning out. It is so much easier to place blame than it is to be 100% fully responsible for the part that you play in what is happening in your life.

Victimhood will strip you of your power the second you give in to its tempting invitation to relinquish responsibility over your life and blame someone or something else for how your life is turning out.

Moving out of victimhood happens when we take radical responsibility for our part in creating a reality that involves a husband who is a jerk, a job we hate, a nosey or gossiping neighbor, or impulsively buying that handbag we love but can't afford. If you're starting to get defensive or feel like you want to write me a letter about how your husband's actions are, in fact, *not* your responsibility, realize that this is how powerful victimhood is and no one gets out of it without first trying to defend themselves and shun responsibility. You may not be responsible for his choices and actions; but you are responsible for inviting him into your life by marriage and choosing to live with him every day. This ongoing choice is what gets you the pleasure of a front row seat to experience all of his choices, live and in action. No one gets out of victimhood without taking radical responsibility in every area of their lives. Not even me.

Every single night that I cried in that room for over a year was about what he said, what she did, and how unfair all of it was. I signed up for "happily ever after" and a ride off into the sunset, not a pilgrimage into the dark night of the soul. I wanted to live free and was distraught that I had to deal with all of this upheaval just to do so. Over the course of one whole year, I shed so many tears that I'm sure I became dehydrated. What I experienced was a death. It felt raw and real and at that time it seemed only negative, but in hindsight I see it for the truth of what it was—a divine blessing. Remember those life-changing words that got me off the floor that night in my son's room? Receiving the powerful message that I was the co-creator of all of this mess catapulted my growth and expansion and proved to be the game-changing moment in my evolution. It was the birth of something new.

In the blink of an eye, your life can change in the most miraculous ways if you are willing to take responsibility for everything in your life. It took me over a year. For some people, it takes an entire life right up until they take their last breath. For others, it takes a few days, or a week. You get to choose how long you keep yourself in the backseat of your own car and how long you want to experience the self-fulfilling prophecy of pain that is victimhood. Your key to freedom lies in liberating yourself by changing the title of your story from *"101 Reasons Why I Never Get What I Want,"* to *"I Create Awesomeness Every Damn Day!"*

Inspired Action

- Make an exhaustive list of your chief complaints in life: the people who annoy you, the things you don't have that you want, the ways you feel held back in life and so on.

  Pour it all out on to the page—even the sticky stuff. Then one by one take responsibility for it. Go down the list and write, "I am responsible for the job that I don't like." "I am responsible for living across the street from that annoying neighbor." Read each one, taking responsibility; and as you read, visualize all of the power that you have given over to these people, things, and situations returning to you. It's time to start reclaiming your precious energy!

Pick Up the Pen

For the first time in my life, I was changing my story from victim to victor. I was about to drive my own car—without all of the noise from the peanut gallery and free of all the limitations, fears, and lack that had now been cleared. I was rewriting the storyline of my life, changing the arc and taking myself down a whole new path. I was literately changing the trajectory of my life and the reality I was living in. Everything in our lives is a reflection of what we believe is possible. So, we can't write a story that runs contrary to our core beliefs.

The stories we tell ourselves about ourselves are often way far off from the truth. They are a reflection of, and a reaction to, the interpretations and conclusions we make very early on about ourselves, others, and life. The themes of our life stories are usually written between the ages of birth and seven years old and we then spend the rest of our lives living them out on our very own stage. The worst part is we don't realize that we have a backspace. At any point you can rewrite, copy and paste, or delete the whole second act of the play!

The body we have, the wealth we have, the people we attract into our lives, the career, the quality of relationships— all of our experiences are a byproduct of what we believe we deserve to experience. For example, I once had a client who led an active lifestyle and had been very happy with her weight most of her life. She felt really good about her body until she had a baby. Then she became unhappy with her weight and couldn't seem to lose the weight she wanted to lose. After a few sessions, we were able to uncover that multiple generations in her family had the same story. The core belief system running through her family is that once you have a child, your body will never be the same.

We have to be sure we aren't living into a story we don't like—and for goodness' sake, that we're not living into someone else's story of who we are. Before we can build a shiny new building to inhabit, we have to make sure the foundation is sound. We have to remove any cracked beliefs that could send the whole thing tumbling down again.

Here are some other very common beliefs that I often see playing out in the lives of my clients:

- "I'll never have enough money."
- "There's something wrong with me."
- "I don't have enough of ______." You can insert any word in the blank.
- "Life is hard."
- "I'm unlovable."
- "I will always struggle with my weight."
- "Other people have it better than me."

The first step in re-writing your story is having the desire to, and the next step is to realize that you have the power to do so, at any moment. This understanding should expand your mind as to what is possible for you instantaneously. Your story can be your greatest asset if you know how to use it to benefit your life, and it can be your biggest downfall if you allow it to keep you stuck.

The day after the bedroom epiphanies, I decided to re-write my future and I started with no idea how to do it. There was no instruction manual, so I turned to a few powerful perspectives and realizations that had awakened within me over the previous few years.

- The first was to surrender and keep surrendering because trying to hold on only kept me feeling rigid and unable to trust and listen.
- The second was to continue releasing from anything that felt icky, old, or stale, and to expand into the things that made me feel amazing.
- And the last was to flow, to be in flow, to meditate on flow, and, if they are serving flow at the local restaurant, to order it.

Inspired Action

- What do you want, my lovely?
- What tickles your fancy, makes your heart skip a beat, and makes you shriek with excitement?
- If you could write the story of the rest of your life, what would it be?
- Take to the page and lay out the vision! Remember, you can have anything and everything that is based in LOVE + TRUTH. Kind of exciting, isn't it?!

Stability is an Illusion

If you like the idea of a good ole' helping of flow, but you're still holding on the idea of a stable life, you will be happy to know that the stability we crave resides within ourselves. Stability never has and never will be something we can find elsewhere. Human beings crave stability. Some of us are very aware of this need and others are not. But when you access deeper and deeper levels of truth about life and within your own being, you realize that nothing is stable. Everything that appears static and material is made of energy; and as we know, energy is always in motion. You are actually far safer in the state of motion than in the illusion of stability. Think about an animal living in the wild. Would it be safer to stay in one place all day long or to move in response to instinct and be present to what's happening in our environment?

The idea that stability, predictability, or complacency is safer than spontaneity and living in present-moment awareness is simply not true. We are part of Mother Nature and we need to move with her flow. A bird that is designed to migrate doesn't get attached to its location. If it did, it would die once the weather changed. It inherently knows that it must migrate in harmony with the changing seasons in order to survive. In the same way, a tree branch that refuses to bend with the wind, breaks. True stability can only be found in movement and growth. Stifling that for decades will wreak havoc on the body, mind, and spirit.

When I realized that the stability I craved could only be created by me, I felt free. I no longer felt that I had to live within the confines that people often erect to keep them feeling safe such as obsessing over retirement accounts, staying in a joyless marriage that gets worse each year, or staying with the career that you never meant to get into—all to guarantee stability. Don't get me wrong. There is nothing wrong with being married, working at a solid career, or saving for a rainy day; but if you are looking to a partner or a paycheck for your internal sense of safety, or saving with the intention of finding lasting stability, you will never find the peace you are looking for. Only when you know that *you* are the source of creating anything and everything in your life and start to do this, can you truly be free. By learning to listen and move with the flow, we become receptive to the universal forces that are in every moment guiding us in the direction of our highest expansion. We are now ready to use our energy to intentionally create.

Finding Flow

When you begin to understand and start living in harmony with the laws of the universe, you open yourself up to what I like to call "The Land of Little Miracles." This is where life starts bringing new people and experiences to you that help you, bit by bit and piece by piece, to discover and fulfill your greatest purpose. Living in flow is acknowledging the paradox that although we don't really control anything, we are all born with the most incredible superpower: we can use our thoughts and feelings to manifest things out of thin air. This may sound pretty darn magical or even far-fetched, but everyone can do this if they are shown how. The right things find us at the right times. When we stop chasing after life, people, and experiences, we begin drawing the right things towards us with our energy rather than with effort. Picture yourself standing still, clear and receptive, and the right things beaming their way to you.

Living in flow means being in the now as much as possible, but not with any judgment when our mind wanders or we feel fear. We understand that the full range of emotions are all a normal part of our human experience, so we don't panic when we make what feels like a wrong turn; we just keep returning to the present moment. It's kind of like riding a wave. There's a rhythm to nature, an ebb and a flow. Know that I give you permission, here and now, to lay down your sword and stop fighting to make things happen. You can start going with the flow instead. I know. It can feel scary to stop; but don't be afraid to occasionally hit the pause button on your outer life in the name of listening to what's really going on within.

Part of releasing is breathing,

getting silent, and finding peace within ourselves, even if there is chaos around us.

Release

Part of releasing is breathing, getting silent, and finding peace within ourselves, even if there is chaos around us. It is also realizing that true stability comes from the connection we forge inside of us. If we keep painting over what doesn't work, the rust will eventually seep through again. This process is not easy, but man is it worth it. What needs to be released? What is no longer serving your life? What feels like it's dragging you down rather than elevating you to a new level? The reflections that follow will support you in this important inquiry.

Inspired Action:
Reflections on Release

Begin by giving yourself permission to slowly and safely "take the lid off" repressed emotions, forgotten desires, or realizations you may have been pushing aside. Then, carve out some time alone or with a qualified coach or a trusted friend, and give yourself space to truly feel what's stirring beneath the surface. A day or two or a week will do to begin the process. Here are some activities that can help you get back in touch with yourself and remain connected to your center no matter what is going on in your outer world:

- Meditation
- Quiet contemplation
- Yoga
- Reading
- Energy work

- Massage
- Reiki
- Going on a spiritual retreat
- Connecting with like-minded people
- Spending time in nature
- Practicing silence
- Connecting to a higher power

After you've given yourself a few weeks of consistently getting quiet and connected within, begin to ask for more clarity about what you would now like your life to look like. You can find clarity gathering questions in the Introspection section at the back of the book.

SECTION III

Experience

Experience

This is the moment where I invite you to breathe deeper than you ever have before, like you are taking in air for two people. And as you exhale, feel your body relax, your shoulders fall, and feel the space within that has been created by all that has been released. Maybe you are not sure if you want to ball your eyes out or if you feel blissfully relieved, or both at the same time. The experience of "going to nothing," of releasing the mental, physical, and emotional blocks that have held you back from your authentic soul expression, has placed you in the perfect position to build anew—even if you have not a clue how to do it. You may feel a little lost, painfully vulnerable, and maybe even a bit like a newbie at life. The soil of your consciousness has been tilled, your values clarified, outworn desires purged, and now new ones begin to come into focus. At this stage in the alchemy, your grip on the past may be softening and and a new willingness to allow life to have its way with you, to express itself through you in new ways.

If you haven't already,
you will soon discover that
the nothingness you are
experiencing after releasing
what is no longer true for you
was never made up of empty
space, but is in fact a fertile
field where new life
can flourish.

If you haven't already, you will soon discover that the nothingness you are experiencing after releasing what is no longer true for you, was never made up of empty space, but is in fact a fertile energetic field where new life can flourish. Sometimes suddenly and sometimes gradually, new possibilities appear on the horizon: an idea, a burning curiosity, or a vision begins to form—and you are magnetically drawn in a new direction. Often this new direction is not "new" at all, but a rediscovery of what you've always been fascinated with or have loved to do since childhood.

Whether you are feeling inclined to quit your job, dye your hair pink, or suddenly become obsessed with saving the whales, the mildly rebellious and yet soulfully connected calling that is resounding inside of you will speak to the core of who you are. Even if your logical mind is telling you

you're crazy, your heart will be cheering you on. You will develop a strange fascination with your mission, as well as a healthy dose of courage to pursue the outrageous, wild, and unthinkable as if it were the next logical step in your life.

People and circumstances who support your new calling will likely start showing up in interesting and synchronistic ways, as the space you created from all that you released begins filling up with new interests and experiences. As the emerging new ideas take root in your mind, you may find yourself wanting to spend all of your free time exploring them. And though the idea may only exist in seed form, eventually you'll begin to catch glimpses of what it could look like if nurtured into full bloom, and you'll feel compelled to start soulfully planting your future.

After the proverbial floor dropped out in my own life, I found it difficult to find solid ground to stand on. This is not everyone's experience of releasing, but it was mine. Sometimes it is difficult to see all of the changes that are happening inside of us. It can feel confusing, strange, and good all at the same time, as any configuration of conflicting emotions are now alive and kicking inside of you. At this point in my own transformation, I could notice some definite changes in how I was living my life. Whereas just a couple of years earlier I used to be a social butterfly and loved to get a new outfit, go out on the town, and rock the dance floor while throwing back a few cocktails, now I found myself wanting to sew a different kind of seed. I wanted to study, learn, and experiment, whip out my magnifying glass to search for unfolding clues on this cosmic scavenger hunt to a high frequency way of living. The path I was being led on was not a social one, but one of deep introspection.

Entire parts of my life began fading away. My career felt distant and slightly uncomfortable, like a relationship that had run its course. And instead of partaking in weekends out on the town, I was deep in the caverns of my inner self. Love was ever present for all people and aspects of my life, yet the energy that bound us to a common reality was shifting. I didn't realize it at the time, but my willingness to feel separate from the only reality that I had ever known, and to surrender to being lost in the abyss, is exactly how I landed on the path back to myself. Sometimes we have to get lost to finally be found.

Sometimes
we have to get lost to finally
be found.

As my life was evolving from monochromatic to electrifying color, I gained a much deeper understanding of and appreciation for why a healthy body is so important. In my past, health was defined almost entirely by diet and exercise in pursuit of a certain exterior appearance; but true physical health not only provides the basis for enjoying all of the sensory experiences available in this dimension of time and space, the body is also the conduit through which powerful, spiritual life force energy can be summoned through us. The healthier it is, the more comfortably it can sustain higher frequencies. I discovered that the more balance I created in my body, the more I was able to access, understand, and accept the truths I was unlocking within. It turns out the greatest adventure of all time was never to be sought out in the world at large, but to be awakened inside of me.

The desire to better understand my awakening sparked an intense curiosity in a wide array of healing methods. While I never intended to hang my hat on any one in particular, I did use what I was learning to affirm the deep inner knowing that was bubbling up within me. For close to a year, I embarked on a journey that I initially believed was one of learning, only to realize that it was actually a multidimensional journey of remembering. It was as if I was now looking at my life from the top of a hill and understanding myself and all that I had lived up to that point in a new context; one that included comprehending each of my experiences as vital pieces of the puzzle. From this higher vantage point, I could see how everything I had experienced was interwoven and part of a grand blueprint for my life. This overview clearly showed me the next steps.

It's as if an updated, "Shanna 2.0" version of me was being born, a version not completely different from who I had been in the past, but an alchemy of my most refined and soul-infused qualities. And so it will be for you, too. As you continue to release the thought patterns and behaviors that are no longer up to speed with what you now want to create, you will begin to get glimpses of the brightest and most expanded version of you—the version that you were born to express.

In the Release phase of the process of transformation, we deconstruct many of the beliefs, expectations and stories that we formerly used to define ourselves, and in so doing, widen the channels through which our creations can be made manifest. As our bodies and minds are freed of toxins in all forms, a higher order of ideas and possibilities begins to surge through us like a lightning bolt. Suddenly we have access to a new set of building blocks, along with greater access to the grandest co-creator of all time, call it God, universal love, source energy, or anything your little heart desires. It is powerful no matter by what name you call it, and it wants to help you create your experience in life purposefully, rather than by default.

When we are blind to the energetic basis of our bodies, minds, and emotions, we are cut off from understanding how to increase the frequency of the energy we are emanating. Our experience of life becomes lackluster. We unconsciously allow the frequency of our lowest emotions and most self-critical perceptions to guide our thoughts, emotions, words, and actions. It's like seeing Wonder Woman walking around depressed, thinking she is powerless, while dressed to the nines with her cuffs and cape. You want to run up to her, tap her on the shoulder, and show her how those badass cuffs work!

Before you can allow the Wonder Woman in you to rise to the fullness of her abilities, you'll have to become conscious of the ways you've been keeping yourself blind to your own superpowers. As I share the following examples of some of the ways I've seen women unwittingly create a less than satisfying experience in relation to their health, finances, relationships, and careers—and the ways I've helped them turn those experiences around—see if you can recognize any of these tendencies operating behind the scenes in your own life.

Nothing But Love

A few sessions into our work together, my client Shelley confided that she could not look at herself in the mirror without putting herself down. She looked right past her beautiful eyes and smooth skin and saw only the parts of her body that she holds negative judgments around: her legs are too short; her nose is too wide; her bottom is too big. And in response to this perception of herself, she would say things to herself internally that she would never utter out loud to another human being. In her own mind, she berated herself with hurtful labels such as "fatso" and "ugly," which naturally caused her to feel ashamed and hopeless about her body. *Saying mean things to yourself,* I suggested gently to Shelley, *is akin to pouring anti-freeze on your garden and wondering why the flowers won't grow.*

Not surprisingly, the more discouraged she felt, the more flaws she found in herself to be discouraged about, and the louder the voice of self-criticism in her head became. Shelley was caught in a cyclical pattern of saying crappy things to herself and breaking her own heart. She created a downward spiral, which can feel difficult, if not impossible, to stop. Inevitably, the frequency generated by this repetitive thought/feeling pattern would drive her to action, but not to an action that would end the pattern or provide the up-leveling her soul was desperately seeking.

When we're circling the drain, things like taking a yoga class or going for a brisk walk don't generally occur to us as a good idea. In those moments, what we have access to are actions that perpetuate the vibe we've already got going on. Like attracts like. So, feeling unhappy with the way she looked and powerless to do anything about it, Shelley would invariably say, "Screw it," and jump in the car to get a burger, fries, and shake. At this point, the momentum of Shelley's thought/feeling pattern had gathered enough speed that she was now compelled to take an external action that was energetically aligned with the frequency she was experiencing within. And until she could find a way to shift out of this low frequency, every choice she made was contained within this loop of negativity.

To affect an external solution,
we had to address the internal source.

It's no wonder that Shelley described her relationship with food, diets, and exercise as being similar to a hamster running faster and faster on a wheel but getting nowhere. To affect an external solution, we had to address the internal source. It is always an inside job. I asked Shelley why she was saying such mean things to herself, and she responded, “Because they’re true.” This was her personal truth about herself that she had constructed a long time ago and was still living in accordance with. And the litany of negative thoughts, feelings, and actions that sprung from this “truth” set the tone for her experience, day in and day out. I asked Shelley if she was willing to work on changing her truth about herself. Happily, she said yes.

To help her make a shift to the positive, I asked Shelley to start deliberately looking for things that she liked about herself every morning—not to lie to herself about a part of her body she was not feeling love for, but to notice the things she genuinely appreciated about herself and to build on that. Within a few short weeks, she was able to recite a list of things that she admired about herself and said that she had come to really look forward to this morning practice. She noticed changes in the way she felt about her body and she also started feeling less suspicious and critical of others. She was making eye contact more often and interacting with people more openly. In the simplest of terms, she began sending herself the energy of love daily, and all aspects of her being were feeling happier and more alive as a result.

To put the potency of negative self-talk into perspective, imagine that you had a family member who was sick with cancer. Would you send that person hate or love? The answer is easy: you would send them love. Even if their body didn’t look good or wasn’t healing as quickly as they would like, you would not send horrible energy their way; you would send compassion. So, why do we think that hating parts of our body is going to help anything? The energy of love is a very high frequency and it has the power to transform the physiology of our bodies. It is truly that powerful!

So, why do we think that hating parts of our body is going to help anything? The energy of love is a very high frequency and it has the power to transform the physiology of our bodies.

You have got to be kind to yourself like you are to everybody else. If you are carrying some extra weight, or experiencing a health challenge or a symptom that is uncomfortable, your body—now more than ever—needs your love. Hateful, critical, judgmental energy does not create an atmosphere that is conducive to healing; in fact, the exact opposite is true. Now, just as I suggested to Shelley, I am not asking you to love parts of your body that you don't love. I'm asking you to find what you do love and actively send love to that part of you in order to allow that energy to build. You may find that the parts that have been hardest to love transform before your eyes in the presence of this beautiful high frequency energy. And, just in case you're wondering.... Yes. Shelley did begin losing weight; not from exercising harder or more often or punishing herself with restrictive meal plans one day, only to rebel against them the next, but as a result of creating a mental and emotional shift in how she saw herself. She found the willingness to change her truth to something more self-affirming. Once this new vibrational tone had been set, her behaviors simply followed suit.

I am certain you have had the experience in your own life that the days when you're feeling stuck in some aspect of your life—a project at work that isn't getting done as quickly as you would like, a nagging awareness that some part of your living space needs revamping, or frustration that, despite your best efforts, you still aren't able to zip those new jeans—the energy of that "stuckness" seems to seep into every other area of your life, even those that are going well. And, I'm sure you've noticed that the reverse is also true: on those days when you experience a breakthrough in some area, even a very small one, the energy that's been liberated breathes new life and new possibilities into every other aspect of your experience. This is because it's the quality of the energy we emanate that becomes the basis of our experience of life and what we ultimately create.

So many people who struggle with excess weight are caught in the same type of downward spiral that Shelley so perfectly describes: negative thoughts trigger negative feelings that culminate in self-sabotaging behaviors. But what's worse is that most people don't even realize this is what's happening. No diet or exercise regime can reverse this tailspin long-term because although the problem manifests externally as weight, the root of the problem is internal.

Inspired Action

Can you pinpoint any areas of your life, including your relationship to food or exercise, where your actions are driven by self-deprecating thoughts and emotions, rather than inspired by self-love and possibility?

- Make a list of those critical thoughts, so that you'll have more choice in the matter of whether or not to act on them when they arise.

The work I do touches every area of a woman's life. When you address and shift something at the level of energy, which is the basis of everything and the very essence of who you are, you come to understand that not only is every aspect of a woman's body interconnected, but every aspect of her life is interconnected as well. When I help someone create more balance and flow in her physical body, the energy that is liberated opens up new possibilities in other areas of her life. It seems weird to think that by changing your food, you set off a domino effect that will change your thoughts, your beliefs, the way you see yourself, and could even potentially manifest a new career, new love, a Mercedes, or a rock pool with a cabana; but it does. So in effect, if you want to manifest a new car and a daily dip in your own pool, do the inner work; change your food and watch new energy and things flow into your life. My client Rebecca offers a powerful case in point.

For The Love of Money

Rebecca came to see me after having struggled with excess weight and low energy much of her adult life. She shared that the feeling of struggle—once seemingly confined only to her experience of her body—was now starting to cloud other aspects of her life, such as the level of joy and enthusiasm she felt in her career. We began making small shifts in her diet and tweaked her sleep patterns, self-care regimen, and dialed in her daily schedule. We worked ultimately to help her restore her energy while simultaneously addressing the imprints of the beliefs she had picked up in childhood regarding her career.

I had her write down all of the things she believed about her career and her ability to earn money. She created a significant list, which made her realize all that she had going on about money. It got even more interesting when I had her write down her parents' beliefs about money and success. It turns out her parents struggled financially throughout her childhood. They were lower-middle class and her father often made fun of "rich" people. She felt embarrassed about her parents in front of other kids, and she felt afraid to ever become one of the people who her father would make fun of. So, playing small in her career was actually protecting her from the pain of being judged by her father. Once these patterns became conscious, she no longer had to live through them, and she became aware of new choices.

Rebecca, who enjoyed a moderately successful career in real estate, had for a decade been selling a few houses a year in the $600,000- $800,000 range in Southern California. About four weeks into our work together, she got a $3,000,000 listing. This far exceeded anything that she had ever sold in the past, and she was as shocked as she was excited.

I share this example because it illustrates so clearly how, when we shift our energy in one area of our lives, such as how we care for our body, it opens the door to a deeper understanding of what is going on under the surface that is robbing us of joy, success, and abundance. Rebecca may have had opportunities around her for years to sell higher -priced properties; but running this old belief system wasn't in resonance with them, so they couldn't become her reality. As she changed her energy frequency, she began resonating with different people and experiences, and new opportunities came to her with almost no effort. In Rebecca's case, the physical opening had not just given her access to more energy; it also allowed more financial abundance to flow into her experience.

As she changed her energy frequency, she began resonating with different people and experiences, and new opportunities came to her with almost no effort.

Experience

Lack and limitation around financial abundance is one of the most pervasive thought patterns of our time. At the core of this perception is a general feeling of "not enough-ness." We usually attribute this feeling to something material that we perceive as lacking in our external world—if only we had X, Y, or Z, we're certain we'd feel better. But in reality, nothing outside of us is sourcing our financial abundance; money is just paper with a whole lot of energy around it. Get your mental energy about this paper flowing in the right direction, and abundance in all forms will be yours.

> *If you fixate* on "I don't have enough money," you will powerfully create that experience.

At the soul level, we fully embody abundance as our birthright. If you have any doubt about this, just observe a young child. She fully and innocently expects her needs to be met, and has no hang-ups whatsoever about asking for and receiving an abundance of love, affection, or nourishment. You can also look anywhere in the natural world and you'll see that lack simply does not exist there either. How many planets are in our solar system, again? And how many solar systems besides our own are out there? Is there any limitation to the sun's power, to the amount of oxygen our bodies can naturally receive, to the number of seeds that sprout into plants, or to the potential of those plants to regenerate? Evidence of our abundance is all around us, but when we are disconnected from this truth, "not enough" becomes our experience, and often these thoughts are centered around money.

If you fixate on "I don't have enough money," you will powerfully create that experience. And as you continue to look through eyes of lack, you'll find it everywhere. We are born with the free will to accept the bounty of this universe and to allow it to flourish in our lives, or to block it from our experience. Look around and you'll see plenty of folks who are actively blocking it. The choice is yours. This has nothing to do with your job, who hasn't paid you back, or the glass ceiling above your head that you constructed with your own hands. If you recite lack, limitation, and not enough-ness daily, sure enough, you'll begin to feel scared, sad, or disappointed in response. And then, if you seek an external fix like getting a new job without first shifting your internal dialogue and beliefs, you will continue to live out the same experience of lack even though you might be making a few more bucks. You just can't out-earn your own internal dialogue; and you can't create outside of your own beliefs.

Once they've bought into a mindset of lack, some women become ridiculously frugal with money, such that they're afraid to spend a dime. Others think, "The hell with it. I'm just going to keep buying things and worry about it later." Some of us go unconscious and completely check out when it comes to managing money or keeping records of spending. The point is that whichever thought/feeling/

action pattern you hold around money will become your experience in that arena of life. You are the c-r-e-a-t-o-r. There is no one else to blame, and no one else to congratulate once you get this spiral heading in the right direction.

When we're in the midst of one of these negative thought-feeling-action tailspins—whether the subject matter has to do with our finances or our health or the welfare of our children—our perception in that moment is that we can't create anything different (and we usually have iron-clad evidence as to why this is so). But the truth is, we created the old pattern, and so too, we can create a new one.

To create what you want in relationship to money, begin by thinking about money as energy and start seeing yourself bringing more of that energy into your life.

To create what you want in relationship to money, begin by thinking about money as energy and start seeing yourself bringing more of that energy into your life. Start thinking about what you can do to increase the energy of money. Do you have ideas for growing your business that feel lucrative to explore, or other areas of interest that you'd like to pursue? The goal here is simply to increase your awareness of and receptivity to the energy of money, and to imagine it flowing more abundantly in your life. If it lights you up to do so, you might visualize your bank account balance growing. Even if right now your balance doesn't have enough zeros behind it, it is a very powerful exercise to think about it increasing, picturing that, and conjuring the feelings that you would associate with the increase.

What would it feel like to have a few million dollars in the bank? What would that allow you to do in your life? Who could you help? What kind of thoughts and ideas would you allow yourself to ponder if finances were not a factor? When the vibration of your dominant thoughts and feelings around money tips into joy and positive expectation, that frequency will inspire your actions, and a new reality around money will be yours. Let's look now at an example of how this same principle applies in relationship to our career expression.

Inspired Action

- How do you perceive or envision the energy of money?
- Do you visualize it as lavish green energy, as the potency of nature, as a feeling of freedom, or as a mandala of ever-widening possibilities?

I invite you to put your pen to the page and free-write any positive associations you have with money—not as a substance, but as an energy. If words feel too constrictive, try doodling, sketching, or coloring. When you are finished put it up on the wall or share it with a friend! The more you intimately connect with the energy and essence of abundance, the more you will discover the abundance that exists all around you.

You Gotta Love What You Do

My client Giselle is a talented performer who had created a very successful career performing in shows that were written by other people. In the course of our work together, I began to sense that she had deeper desires than her current starring role allowed her to express. When I asked about this, she shared that she had always wanted to perform in a show that she had written herself, and that the prospect of being at the creative source of a project was thrilling to her. And then, in almost the same breath, she shared that although she wanted this, she was very afraid to pursue it. What would people think? Is she as good of a writer as she is a performer? Would her peers accept her work?

Giselle had a host of excuses as to why it was probably in her best interest to stay put, even though her desire was clearly pulling her in a new direction. Artists in particular often have great hesitation when considering making the leap to a new area of self-expression after having found success in another; but concerns like these come up for everyone in every career across the board.

Over the years, I've worked with clients who start out in a field they love, and may even create a good measure of success in it. And then at some point they realize they are ready to grow and are called to do something else. Like Giselle, women who are experiencing this career discontent will often start having nagging thoughts about their career, such as, *I don't love what I do*, *It's not fun anymore*, or—as those thoughts escalate—*Is this it? Is this all my life is ever going to be?* And, as time goes on, they may even start to voice those complaints to anyone around them who will listen.

The feelings associated with these thought patterns can range from frustration and annoyance to despondency and resignation, and we will seek relief from these negative emotions through some course of action (or, as the case may be, through inaction). We may come home from work each day and tune out to late night reruns or take up an addiction to fine chocolates; or better yet, reruns while popping chocolates and washing it down with wine (there she goes again with that wine thing!). Mentally, we might really desire to make a change, but lack the motivation to seek out a new career. So instead of taking action towards creating the career we want, we create ourselves staying stuck instead, and the pattern repeats year after year. Giselle initially came to me to lose weight and feel better. I knew that once we could get her to other side of her habitual thought patterns and fears, she'd begin to hear her soul frequency more clearly and find all the confidence and creativity she'd need to follow her calling.

It is interesting how many times we think that weight is the source of our problems and once that gets fixed, all will be roses and daffodils.

It is interesting how many times we think that weight is the source of our problems and once that gets fixed, all will be roses and daffodils. But there is always a bigger conversation going on anytime someone is dealing with unwanted weight. As Giselle began to heal her body by giving it the vital nutrients it needed to thrive, her confidence did grow and she lightened her body, but that is not what ultimately led to the long-term results of roses and daffodils. Our bodies are constantly seeking homeostasis, which means anytime we are carrying extra pounds, weight loss is always trying to happen. If you reduce the amount of toxins, increase nutrients, and eat high frequency fuel, you will see results, but keeping those results only happens with taking care of yourself in other ways: by allowing great energy to grow and expand within you. Losing weight is not the end game. Shifting and expanding your energy to support a new way of being that has you take amazing care of yourself is where it's at.

As your internal set point changes, you will crave great fuel and will naturally desire a certain amount of movement in your body daily. Is it a slow process? It can be, depending on how much blocked energy has accumulated and how resistant you are to allowing it to flow. But once I help a woman become more sensitive to her own soul frequency, energy starts moving, and steadily builds momentum, like a train that chugs slowly at first and is soon booking it down the track. The connection to your own resonance happens quickly for some and takes longer for others; either way it is powerful and life-altering.

As Giselle noticed movement toward her desire to look and feel better, she found more movement in her mind as well. Ideas started percolating, and unlike before, she had both the inclination and the energy to write them down. She began keeping a notepad with her wherever she went—even at the gym—and simply set the intention to become open to receive. Ideas are all around us, but it's our receptivity to them that makes all the difference. In fact, you could say that receptivity and creativity are two sides of the same coin. And once we have received the idea, the universe will point us in all the right directions to bring it to fruition.

Losing weight is not the end game.

Shifting and expanding your energy to support a new way of being that has you take amazing care of yourself is where it's at.

Giselle slowly began to realize the power of her superhero cape as she sat in front of her computer, gold cuffs and all, and wrote from her heart. The project was not without growing pains, but when it was done, the show she had envisioned creating was on the page. A year later, when Giselle stood center stage for her final bow, in the show she had written, in front of a packed audience who were all on their feet, she knew, in that moment, that her life would never be the same. She had slain her own dragon and came out the other side a new woman. When we tune into our soul frequency, rather than the frequency of limitation, doubt, and fear, we begin to discover who we are at the deepest level—beyond our own ego constructs and the concerns about the opinions of others. We begin to love ourselves enough to listen to and really honor who we are and what we need. Having emptied ourselves of the need to seek control or prove worthiness, we are free to meet each moment, every person and experience with curiosity.

Along the path to locating your unique soul frequency, you are going to ruffle your own feathers and, to some degree, the feathers of everyone in your life.

Along the path to locating your unique soul frequency, you are going to ruffle your own feathers and, to some degree, the feathers of everyone in your life. Call it an initiation of sorts that tests your commitment to yourself. If you've made it this far in this book, then you are ready and I assure you that you don't need anyone else's permission, admiration, or acceptance to begin deliberately creating your life. It is in this open space that specific creation can occur, and in the same way that nature abhors a vacuum, life will take full advantage of your spaciousness. "Career" ceases to be only a means of making money or achieving status, and becomes an ever-evolving vehicle through which you can enjoy your unique talents and share your wisdom and your gifts.

The path to creating the career that you want will unfold naturally as you allow yourself to connect with what you really want to be doing in the world. What lights you up? What inspires you? What gives you a sense of fulfillment at the end of a day? Most people choose their career path based on what others want for them, on societal pressures, or on the promise of financial gain. Many women settle on a career that is very well known simply because they don't know what else is possible. Most of us have not yet keyed into what our unique gifts are and what field would best allow those gifts to be expressed.

For many of the women I work with, career has yet to become a natural extension of self. Their realm of career possibility does not include what will make them feel fully self-expressed. They do not consider that the things we're meant to do in this life come to us almost effortlessly. In fact, our unique gifts often come so easily that, like water to fish and air to birds, we can't distinguish them as anything special. Add to this the fact that many of us were taught that hard work is the price that must be paid to earn compensation, and it's understandable why it may seem unfair or impossible to be compensated at a high level for something that we truly enjoy and that comes so easily.

The piece that's missing in this belief system is that what comes easily to you doesn't necessarily come easily to others, and that you are meant to give that gift away and in return be supported in sustaining your life. Almost everyone I work with who comes seeking assistance in releasing a physical manifestation of blocked energy taps into a deeper level of creativity and greater access to their gifts through the process of working together. They start to see what's possible within them, and they start to feel called to help people in their own unique way.

> **Truth comes through**
> in the funniest, most ironic,
> and piecemeal of ways,
> leaving us wondering at times
> what it all means.

I promise you that when the words "LOVE + TRUTH" began taking up residence in my consciousness, I could never have guessed that they would arrive in order to take me on a journey that would culminate in me finding a career expression that not only serves others in such a powerful and life-changing way, but inspires me to be in the world as my most intuitive, authentic, and compassionate self. Truth comes through in the funniest, most ironic, and piecemeal of ways, leaving us wondering at times what it all means. But I assure you that as you engage in this inquiry, take whatever actions you are inspired to take, and remain open to new possibilities that occur to you, you are deliberately causing a shift in the matrix, and even small steps will be rewarded. You're putting a higher frequency of energy out into the Universe, and this energy *must* come back to you.

Inspired Action

Begin thinking about how you want your career to look and feel, and how you want it to expand. Allow your thoughts and feelings to linger in that possibility.

- What's the coolest thing you can imagine doing with your particular talents and skillset?

- What wisdom has life given you firsthand, and how thrilling would it be to pass that wisdom on to others?

Go about this mental exercise with the intention to simply get the train rolling. Once a strong enough pattern of thought and feeling is created, you won't be able to stop yourself from taking action on it. We can only contemplate good feelings, thoughts, and emotions for so long before they naturally compel us into action. And I encourage you to swim out with whatever idea lands in your awareness, even if it seems silly, because your linear mind has no clue and no ability to predict where it might lead.

Finding True Love

Last but not least, and maybe even the most important since it touches our lives in so many ways, let's look at how we unconsciously mis-create in the realm of our intimate relationships. Relationships are so central to our life experience because they provide a direct platform for expressing and receiving love—and yet many single women who would like to create a great relationship sabotage this desire with beliefs such as "all of the good ones are taken" or "it's too much trouble" or by convincing themselves that they don't look right, act right, or attract the right people. Likewise, many women who are already in relationships spend the lion's share of their time with their partners frustrated or angry over dirty socks, unpaid bills, or inattentiveness; and the fairytale first kiss days of their relationship are but a distant memory.

Over time, the theme song of the relationship goes from "You Light Up My Life" to "You Don't Bring Me Flowers Anymore"—and, as we've seen throughout this section, we cannot entertain thoughts like these without causing a similar frequency of feelings, probably somewhere in the range of loneliness, anger, sadness, or fear. And, as we've also seen in the previous examples, this thought/feeling pattern will eventually culminate in an action: some women will withdraw and give up. Some may throw a look to their mate that could turn water into ice. Some will haphazardly throw themselves into a series of bad relationships in an unconscious attempt to prove their worldview about men—or partnership in general—is right.

And, of course, all of this is happening at a subconscious level. At a conscious level, all you are aware of is that when you go to a party or come home from work, you are either ignored or celebrated by your partner. What you may not realize is that if you subconsciously believe that your partner is a jerk or that it's too late in your life to be happily in love, then that's the experience you will continually create. These are just limitations and blocks about being in relationships, and when this is the energy we are sending out, it hinders any new experience from coming in. It's not that those people aren't out there or that your relationship with your partner can't be awesome. It's just that nothing we want can find its way in when there is static in our energy frequency or we are living out of beliefs that block the free flow of love.

When you open up your energy and clear out the beliefs and patterns of thought that stand in the way of creating a loving relationship, the right person will show up in your life, or your current partner will become it with little to no effort. There won't be the typical hemming and hawing about whether or not he is "the one" or if this partnership is "working out." You'll know because you'll feel it—not in your solar plexus as that familiar pang of longing or angst, but as a calm, clear knowing. Having a great relationship requires one to polish the cuffs, iron the cape, and stand in one's full worth and power. We attract what we think we deserve. And you, my dear, deserve a deep, soulfully connected, supportive, and loving relationship!

As you continue to increase the energy of your thoughts and feelings around creating true love, you will begin to invite new people into your life who resonate at the same level. You will feel resonance with their energy to the degree that you are in touch with your own soul frequency. Relationships that are based in something other than love—such as dependency or habit—are not going to resonate at the soul frequency. And often, in making a stronger commitment to our own evolution, we may be called to let go of relationships that we've outgrown.

When we first started working together, my client Skye was in a marriage that she described as being over a long time ago, but she didn't feel ready to officially end it. So, rather than make a decision, she saw no harm in allowing the relationship to linger. After years of living in this sort of impasse, Skye started experiencing physical symptoms in the form of exhaustion and occasional tension headaches. She implemented my suggestions for cleaning up her diet and added in some key nutrients, but she was still experiencing physical symptoms. It didn't take long to put these pieces together: her intuition was telling her that the relationship was over, and the longer she ignored this inner truth, the more discord she was creating within herself.

In the course of working together, I explained to Skye that the physical body often manifests the pain stored in our mental, emotional, and spiritual bodies because we usually don't honor these more subtle aspects of our being until a more acute physical ailment forces us to pay attention. In the short term it may seem easier to endure an uncomfortable symptom than it is to face the prospect of making significant life changes; but in the long run we are only delaying the inevitable.

The only thing that ever stands in the way of acknowledging our deeper truth and taking action on it is the fear of change. Stepping into our power and actually taking a stand to create what we want in life is way scarier for most people than it is to stay stuck in the familiar that isn't that great. Throughout our time together, Skye came to understand this principle and, in her own time, found the faith to transition out of her relationship. As she did, her tension and lack of energy was replaced with a new zest for life—and, eventually, a new relationship with a man who is a much better match.

As an aside, I think it's important to point out that Skye made these changes in her own time and from her own awareness. We get where we get in life in our own divine time, and I'm a firm believer that no one should ever push us to make a choice that we're not ready for. As long as we're aware of what's going on and conscious of the consequences of the choices we are making, then we should listen to our own inner guidance and apply the power of our own free will to decide if and when a new choice should be made.

I often get asked if stories like the ones I have shared throughout this section are just a coincidence, and my answer is that there are no coincidences. Everything that comes to us or does not come to us is in direct response to the energy that we put out into the world. The things that we chalk up to coincidence are just a reflection of our own transmission of energy being returned to us in many different ways, at different times, and through different people.

I hope you are beginning to get the essence of what each of these stories conveys: that everything that eventually becomes a physical circumstance begins as a sequence of thoughts and emotions, which, like a pinball, can only travel within the channels of our already-established beliefs. As we explored in the previous section, these ruts in our thinking are created by our previous experiences. And they are further narrowed by energy that is blocked when we avoid emotions we don't want to feel. There are infinite choices and therefore infinite possibilities available to all of us, but the realities that we create for ourselves always land within the framework of what we believe is possible. The great news is that because every human being exists in a constant state of becoming, the framework of what is possible for us can always be expanded.

The more willing you are to follow your own inner compass as it guides you in the direction of greater balance and joy, the more confidence you will develop in your ability to chart your own course, even if you are not sure where its winding turns will lead. Because you trust yourself to be the caretaker of your own wellbeing, you will feel at home wherever you go and walk with the certainty that whatever obstacles may temporarily cast a shadow over your light, your connection with yourself can always guide you back to your truth. But, if you are freaking out, in a panic, or about to lose your mind because the prospect of change is overwhelming, or if you feel frozen by fear like a deer in headlights, you are not alone. You are in very good company.

Inspired Action

Whether you are seeking a relationship or are currently in one, begin to identify the dominant thoughts, perceptions and attitudes you hold about this aspect of your life.

- Do you generally feel positive and expectant, or resigned and resentful?
- What is the "story" you are playing in your head about love?

Mind the Gap

Please don't throw your hands in the air and decide this transformation stuff is not the path for you. Please don't go running for the nearest exit door. There is no going back to your not-so-fulfilling-but-comfortable past reality, as much as that might appeal to you at this point. Once you're awake, you can't just pass out on the floor again in ignorant bliss. In order to board the train to the authentic you, you have to be mindful of the gap between releasing the old and creating a new experience. The gap is a necessary pause and recalibration of your energy system. Take a moment, but don't park yourself on the platform watching your train pass you by. No one wants to be stuck in an underground tunnel indefinitely. It's dark, a little musty, and can be dangerous to your psyche. Minding the gap requires a deep breath, some real fortitude, and the willingness to begin anew. It can feel like everything around you is in chaos and you just want to pick up the pieces and put them all back together; but hold on! Something new and better is being created within you.

When I was waiting on that metaphoric platform, I had days when I wanted to run back to the cushy life I had known. There were days I felt lost, days I cried, days I felt stuck, and whole weeks where I didn't know how the heck I ended up in this tunnel in the first place. This kind of drama happens in movies and to other people, I thought; not to me. Eventually, though, I came to accept my new reality. Here are some of the tips that helped me get out of the tunnel and onto the right train.

- I began by saying YES to opportunities, even when they scared me, even when they felt too expensive, even when they weren't convenient, and especially when my intuition was nudging me in that direction. The word YES was like a doorway into new experiences, new people, a new business, and a new life. I YESSED my way through the fear because I knew that if I kept my energy flowing in a positive direction in the form of thoughts and feelings that it would be impossible for me not to take action. And through action, my intentions would expand and manifest.

- I did not wait until I was sure about everything (never going to happen). I did not ask permission from those living in fear (never going to be supportive), and I did not look for reasons why it would not work (never going to create greatness while you are busy creating doubt, limitation, or fear). What I *did* do was hire the right people who knew what I didn't know (leveraged the brilliance of others). I invested almost every dollar I had, and it was not a lot at first, in myself and developing my talents (I did not blow money on the latest fashions, expensive dinners or things that don't really matter), and I became relentless in my intention to help people heal (you have to have a powerful intention).

Where going to nothing feels big, vast, and oftentimes painful, the gap feels like apprehension disguised as lack of direction. So if you're thinking, I *am not sure what to do* or, *I have no idea how to start*, my advice is don't wait to get it right. Just start with anything that makes your heart sing.

Do something different than you have ever done before. Move the energy in your life from stagnant and methodical to free flowing and eclectic. Get outside of the box, where life beyond your current reality is happening. We discover a new way to think when we are awake in the spontaneity of life, not asleep in the monotony. To make your way out of the gap, look for ways to broaden your horizons, which will help you start redirecting your thoughts to begin creating the new.

Inspired Action

- Let's shake things up a bit! Getting outside of the box in big and small ways is important, necessary, and very fun. Whether it is driving a new route to work, taking a new yoga class or going on a blind date, it is time to bring in new energy by switching things up. Start with one small and one big "get outside of the box moment" this week—and level up from there!

The Creation Equation

Raise your hand if you hate math. Who passed notes, doodled, or went on a mental vacation during algebra or geometry class? I certainly did and yet, the equation you're about to learn is one you are going to want to memorize and use for the rest of your life. It's what I call the "Creation Equation." Now that we've looked at real-life examples of how, by virtue of the frequency of our most dominant thoughts and feelings, we sometimes create the exact opposite of what we want, let's break down the process of how creation actually occurs—whether it's the creation of an experience that is wanted or the creation of one that is unwanted.

Remember, everything that exists in the tangible world is created first in the invisible realm of an idea. As the idea is shared and expressed, the energy of this idea picks up momentum and grows into a physical reality through a number of predictable steps. Let's take a look at the three main factors that are at work behind every act of creation. Then we can explore the mechanics of each component. When you understand this formula and become a rock star at applying it deliberately rather than by default, you will have unlocked within you the power to create any experience you desire.

THE CREATION EQUATION:

THOUGHT + FEELING + ACTION = EXPERIENCE

As we saw in the examples of the women who so generously shared their stories here, the creation of any experience begins with a thought, whether it's something tangible like a new car, or something intangible like falling in love or feeling confident. When this thought first occurs, it might be fully formed (i.e., *I love my son!*). Or, it might arise as a subtle inkling, like a general feeling of interest (i.e., *Maybe I want to look at wallpaper for the bedroom*). It could also feel like the pleasure you get when something bright or beautiful captures your attention, like a rose on your daily walk. However vague or well-developed they are, our thoughts represent the beginning point of everything we create in our lives.

As educator and author Stephen Covey brilliantly explains in *The 7 Habits of Highly Effective People,* "All things are created twice, first in the mind and then in reality." Once a thought occurs to us, we get to choose whether to nourish its continued growth by feeding it with our attention, or to allow it to die of natural causes by withdrawing our attention from it. Remember that where attention goes, energy flows. The more we contemplate a small thought, the bigger and more defined it becomes; and like the branches of a tree, one thought continues to give rise to another until the tree's branches span across the sky and its roots anchor deep in the ground.

Whether we create something wanted or unwanted depends on the frequency of our thoughts.

Like every other aspect of us, our thoughts are comprised of energy, and this energy is at the basis of everything that we can potentially create. Whether we create something wanted or unwanted depends on the frequency of our thoughts. The energy of our thoughts range in frequency from very light, high, unrestricted thoughts that feel fabulous when we think them, to low, dark thoughts that make us feel awful or even paralyzed. Thoughts are the currency of creation.

A Penny for Your Thoughts

Our thoughts exert a profound influence over the quality of our experience. A Japanese author and researcher named Dr. Masaru Emoto confirmed this dramatically through conducting experiments with water to examine the effect that thoughts have on physical reality. He chose water as the focus of his research, both because water has an amazing ability to hold and transfer information and because the results of his research would also apply to human beings, given that our bodies are made primarily of water.

In the experiments, petri dishes containing small samples of water were deliberately exposed to particular thoughts, words, and images — some of which were soothing and healing, and others, which were violent or hateful. Immediately following this exposure, Emoto and his team quickly froze the water samples and examined the ice crystals that formed in each one. What they discovered was remarkable and is now documented as pictures in Emoto's best-selling book, *The Hidden Messages in Water.*

In short, the water samples that were exposed to loving and harmonious thoughts and intentions like "I love you" and "you're beautiful," froze into crystals that looked like well-organized, symmetrical snowflakes. Those that were exposed to violent or hateful thoughts, such as "I hate you" and "you're ugly," did not form into snowflakes; they froze into jagged, chaotic sprays of water. Emoto's experiment accomplished what he had set out to do; proving that every thought, word, and intention we offer holds a unique energy frequency that is powerful enough to change the molecular structure of the water in our bodies.

Of course, this is great news if the thoughts we routinely think are positive, life affirming, and bring joy and value to others and ourselves; but oftentimes, this is not the case. Our minds are actually geared towards the negative, and while most of us do not enjoy negative thoughts, we become accustomed to them all the same. The most magnificent part of being human is that at any moment in time, you can change your thoughts, transform the water formations inside of you, and send off chemical reactions in your body that can change your experiences and the course of your life. That, my friend, is a miracle and that miracle is YOU!

Inspired Action

Tracking your thoughts for thirty minutes is a powerful exercise to discover the paths that your mind most commonly wanders down. Set a timer and lay down in silence. Notice what thoughts pop up. Every single thought is the beginning of creating something in your life.

- Are your current thoughts in alignment with what you want to create?

Find Your Groove

If Barry Manilow is not your speed and Vanilla Ice on replay is painful, you will have to pick a new record to play in your head. And to do this, you'll have to go against the grain of many of the mindsets that were passed down to you. From a very early age, we are trained by those around us to notice what's wrong, what's missing, and what could be better. Like Shelley, we may notice and dwell on our own imperfections, but just as often, we direct our negative thoughts toward others. *"Look at how that jerk is driving! I can't believe she's wearing that. This place sure has gone downhill."* These may seem like innocent or even comical observations; but from an energetic standpoint, they are much, much more.

Each thought is building momentum towards an eventual outcome. The more we permit dark, doubtful, or critical thought patterns to run rampant in our minds like crappy outdated songs, the more familiar to us they become; and soon our brain is stuck in a worn groove, playing the same annoying tunes over and over again.

Thoughts become things, and the things they become reflect the frequency that is most dominant within us at every phase of unfolding.

Thoughts become things, and the things they become reflect the frequency that is most dominant within us at every phase of unfolding. For example, imagine that you have an upcoming event—a milestone birthday you want to acknowledge, a significant personal or career accomplishment you'd like to celebrate, or even an event you are in charge of coordinating at work. Long before that event ever takes place in real-time, it manifests first as an idea and then as a sequence of thoughts. How it will ultimately turn out when it manifests as a three-dimensional experience in time and space, has *everything* to do with the frequency of the thoughts you offer about it while it is in the process of becoming. This is because every thought generates within us a correspondent feeling, and once this occurs, the creative power of our thoughts is exponentially multiplied. This evolution represents the next step in the Creative Equation—feelings—which are the spark that lights a fire underneath your thoughts.

The Spark

Imagine that you just had a thought that you'd really love to start your own business. Now, in actuality, your acknowledgment of that singular thought has already set the creative process into motion; but where you take it from this point has *everything* to do with what you will ultimately create.

For the sake of this example, imagine that you've made a decision to take this whole energy frequency mumbo-jumbo thing out for a real-life test drive. You're open to the possibility that thoughts really do become things, and you've decided to take a shot at using the power of your thoughts to create your own business. Knowing what you know now, about how one thought branches out into another until a proverbial tree is created, as soon as that original thought occurs in your mind, you begin deliberately scanning your experience for other thoughts that resonate with this "tree" that you want to create in the area of your career.

> Your creation
> is now crossing the threshold that separates the invisible realm of potentiality from the manifested world of form.

Maybe you decide to ask yourself some of the questions I posed earlier in this section: "What is it about starting my own business that lights me up? Why does this idea inspire me? If I had it all my way, where would I want my business to be? How would I like it to look?" As you ask questions and make yourself receptive to the answers, your original thought will expand into two or three thoughts, until your thoughts about this new idea are as solid and well-formed as the branches of a giant tree. If you allow this creative process to keep rolling, without slamming on the brakes by diverting your attention to doubts or dwelling on what you might lack, the thoughts about your ideal business will continue to gain momentum. At some point right around here, a tipping point will occur. Your thoughts will begin producing feelings in your body that resonate with their same high frequency. You are now experiencing feelings like excitement, possibility, inspiration, and exhilaration; and the spark that these feelings add to the Creative Equation have the same effect as adding rocket fuel to a raging fire.

Soon you are experiencing thoughts and feelings in such a rapid-fire sequence that you can't tell which came first—because in truth they are now operating in a continuous loop: your high frequency, positive thoughts are creating more good-feeling emotions, and those good-feeling emotions are inspiring more high-frequency thoughts. Ten thoughts, ten feelings... ideas are popping like Cristal Champagne at a Vegas nightclub and you are feeling more and more expansive. As you allow this creative process to continue to increase in momentum, it begins to take on what can only be described as a life of its own. And when I say it takes on "a life of its own," I mean it takes up residence in YOUR life. Your creation is now crossing the threshold that separates the invisible realm of potentiality from the manifested world of form: the combined force of the energy of your thoughts and emotions propels you undeniably into action.

Rays of Light

At this point in the Creative Equation, you literally and figuratively cannot contain yourself. The combined energy of your high-flying thoughts now fuel-injected with high-flying feelings is not content to remain only in the invisible realm of thought and emotion. This idea is seeking to be physically manifested, through immediate birth into the tangible world of people, objects, experiences, and things, and it has chosen *you* as its mother. If you've ever been pregnant—with a child or an idea or a cause—you know the powerful forces that this impending event summon both within you and through you. Your nesting urge is on overdrive; you know exactly why you have been chosen as the guardian of this creation, and you know for certain that life has prepared you perfectly for the task.

You have a baby on the way—a fresh, beautiful, life-giving, breath-of-fresh-air contribution to Planet Earth—and there is no freaking question as to whether or not you are going to take the steps to prepare for its birth. You are off and running in every sense of the term. You scramble for a notepad only to find that you can't write fast enough. Mentally, you're receiving images of logos and business cards, and next steps continue to occur while you're on the phone with that friend who mentioned subletting office space the other day.

One action is leading naturally and effortlessly to the next, and the whole experience is exhilarating. You are walking in a ray of inspirational, awe-inspiring, and radiant light that is opening a vortex that more and more ideas and experiences get drawn into. Doors open, connections are made, things get checked off your list, and voila, your vision has become a reality. Your baby, your creation, that wisp of an idea that started as all things do—as a single, unobstructed, uncontested thought—has now manifested as your EXPERIENCE.

These three steps of the Creative Equation—thoughts, which lead to feelings, which inspire us to action—are at work in all situations and all things, and we are always applying them whether we are aware of it or not. And what's really fascinating is that the same exact three steps create wanted experiences just as easily as unwanted ones. They can create you getting fired, gaining weight, sabotaging a relationship, or being broke just as easily as they can manifest you starting a business, losing weight, falling in love, or getting rich. What they create is up to each one of us. You have the choice to live on a downward spiral or on an upward spiral. Our thoughts, feelings, and actions hold the power to create or destroy us physically, mentally, and emotionally, which is why it is vital to become conscious of the frequency of energy that we're generating within ourselves—and to become determined to do something about raising that frequency in every area of our life, starting right here and right now.

In coming to understand the creative process, you reclaim the power to use it consciously rather than by default. This holds the key to redirecting your life towards the expression of the truest version of yourself and to giving you the power to create daily the experiences that you desire. Let's agree that creating what you don't want sucks; and now that you know you can create what you *do* want, let that just simmer within your psyche. Really, it is going to take a minute, a day, a week, a month, or maybe even a year to let this truth wash over you and seep into every crevice of your mind. Then, you are going to have to get used to believing this with every multidimensional aspect of your being.

Your question right now may be, HOW do I do this, Shanna? And my answer is, it begins with a thought, which is fueled by feelings, which inspire action, and finally, you know that your creation is reality because you have experienced it on mental, emotional, and physical planes. And in that moment, you become conscious of your vast ability to create, which means you will never see yourself or your life the same way again.

You'll understand that you can never change your experience by trying to change people or circumstances outside of yourself. To affect this change, you must go within.

With this knowledge and a little practice at applying it, you will find yourself suddenly sprung loose from the backseat and into the driver's seat of your life. You'll understand that you can never change your experience by trying to change people or circumstances outside of yourself. To affect this change, you must go within. Once backstage and behind the drawing board, you can refine and rescript your life experience until it perfectly reflects your heart's desires. As you change YOU, the movie of your life, complete with its colorful cast of characters, changes in response, and a whole new reality is projected on the screen. Within this simple formula lies the understanding of how every human being creates his or her own reality. When you drop your issues with math and apply this equation daily, others won't know how you did it, won't believe what you created, and they won't even recognize you. You will be transformed.

Inspired Action
Reflections on Experience

The first step in mastering the art of intentionally directing energy in order to create the outcomes you desire is to become aware of the frequency of your most dominant thoughts, feelings, moods, and attitudes. The practice below will first help you get a handle on how you are currently flowing your creative energy. If you want support on how to begin flowing it more positively and deliberately, check out the Introspection section at the back of the book.

- Take twenty minutes a day to examine the well-worn paths that your mind tends to automatically travel down. For example, with regard to your relationship with food, weight, and your body, are your thoughts primarily positive or negative?

- How often do you say mean things to yourself or pick yourself apart when you look in the mirror?

- How often do you compliment yourself for your unique skills and talents, or pat yourself on the back for really showing up even if your efforts didn't produce the desired outcome?

The answers to these questions will reveal how you are directing the power of your attention, and will help you make the correlation between the quality of energy you are flowing into each important aspect of your life and the harvest you are reaping as a result.

SECTION IV

Align

Align

Ahh, at last we've arrived to the phase of transformation that seals the proverbial deal—which is why it's usually the part we most want to skip. I equate the act of aligning to something I call the "Tile Floor Syndrome." Let me explain.

Suppose you have decided to have some beautiful stone tile flooring installed in your kitchen and living room, and that you wish to continue living in your home during this mini-remodel. The project begins, and soon your house is filled with workmen, dust, and the unbearably loud screeching noise of a tile saw firing up every few minutes. Most of your belongings are piled up in other rooms, covered in plastic and inaccessible.

At the onset of this beautification project, you found all the commotion rather exciting; but after two weeks you are thoroughly "over" the whole process and wondering at this point if you really needed new flooring in the first place. Then, on the day the workmen set the final tile, as you breathe a sigh of relief and are ready to begin moving your furniture back into place, the foreman tells you that the crew needs to come back in three days to apply a coat of sealant to the floor.

Annoyance rises quickly to the surface. It has been two weeks for goodness' sake, and the floors look great as they are. You're done putting your life on hold and just want to get back to business as usual. So, you skip the sealant, telling yourself that it's probably just a scam and the floors don't need it anyway. Plus, you don't have three more days to wait because *that* is an eternity and there is way too much on your calendar already. So, you thank the crew for their work and send them hastily on their way.

A year later, however, after your holiday party, you wake up and find two red wine stains and as you start to inspect your floor a little closer, you see that your beige grout is now a dingy brown in the high traffic areas. You scrub to no avail, and you call to complain to the company. Anger again boils within you when they remind you that you chose not to seal the floors, which would have kept the tiles from becoming discolored. But this is not the end of the bad news: now that so much time has passed, they say, the fix is no longer as simple as applying sealant. They need to come and treat the entire floor, wait the same three days you initially told them not to, and apply the sealant. In retrospect, you now really wish you would have sucked it up, been patient, and had the tile sealed in the first place; but instead of owning that your impatience created this unwanted outcome, you find yourself lashing out at the tile guy.

> **It's human nature** to want to cut corners; we'd all like to put in 80% of the effort and get a 100% result.

Now, obviously, this example has nothing to do with tile floors. It is actually a story about alignment. It's human nature to want to cut corners; we'd all like to put in 80% of the effort and get a 100% result. Well, in the context of transformation, alignment is the missing 20% that feels unimportant, like too much trouble, or occurs to us—as in the example about flooring tile—as not even being necessary, so we gloss over it (no pun intended; gloss is not the same as sealant!) instead. There is something about the final stretch where the human mind resists going all of the way because to go all the way usually means we are going to break through a preconceived belief or limitation.

In the tile floor story, the breakthrough was about patience, and not prioritizing short term convenience over long term results. This glossing over is the phenomenon behind why people go on diets and end up putting all the weight they lost right back on. Momentarily satisfied with the aesthetic improvement, they skip the most important part by failing to adjust their lifestyle in such a way that makes it possible to sustain the changes they made.

In our attempts to save a little time, money or effort, we end up costing ourselves so much more of all of the above—not to mention disappointment and frustration—all because we were unwilling go all the way the first time. Aligning with and deliberately maintaining the improvements we've made is always a more energy-efficient approach than starting over time and time again. And yet, we resist it around every corner. We tend to want to quantum leap to the final destination and skip over the important lessons and insights that reveal themselves along the way. We don't want to wait to seal the floor, or take the time to anchor in our new frequency through alignment. It seems easier to skip steps and leap to the finish line. It is the tortoise and the hare story all over again. You know who makes it to the finish line first, the slow and steady gal with the shell.

When you build the foundation in any area of your life slowly and incrementally, while guarding it and keeping it pure each time someone or something could cause it to go sideways, you are in a better position to maintain your results than you would be, had someone just *presto!* given it to you. It's like the girl who wins the lottery and bleeds money until, in very short time, she is right back where she started. Unless we expand our inner set point at our own rate and in our own time, we will not be able to maintain any new outer manifestation for very long. Just as those new tile floors could not maintain their shine without sealant, you will not fully integrate a manifestation without alignment. You have to take the time to do it right. That is how we seal the deal.

In understanding the Creation Equation, you've learned that you can tap into your innate ability to consciously design your experience in each key aspect of your life by raising the energetic frequency of your most dominant thoughts, feelings, and actions. And as you apply this formula, you'll begin to really understand that energy is truly the basis of everything. The quality of the energy you *breathe* into each one of your goals and desires is always reflected back to you in the quality of the results you create. If you want to create results that last, you have to become willing to go that final 20% with more intention, importance, and focus than you applied to the first 80%. Lifelong success in any area of life can only happen when we maintain a consistent state of alignment.

Now, if this conversation is suddenly making you tired, I completely understand. It's natural to encounter some internal resistance when you discover the energetic focus necessary to be consistent and sustain the changes you want to make. If this is the case, I recommend that you give yourself permission to go to bed and pick this book back up when you are ready to rock and roll with every ounce of you. To ALIGN is *that* important.

Choose Wisely

When you reclaim your original soul frequency, its resounding note reverberates in every aspect of yourself and through every corner of your life. This brings about change on all dimensions. That which is in harmony with the note of your soul moves more powerfully into your life, while that which vibrates in opposition or discord gradually or dramatically ceases being a part of your experience. To maintain your soul frequency and sustain the high vibration you have achieved, you will need to align yourself with people, nourishment, and experiences that support this energy, while allowing the people and experiences that are not in resonance to fall away. Just like bio hackers use nutrition, nutrigenomics, and lifestyle changes to take control of their human biology, it is time to start frequency hacking your life by taking control of the energy that you interact with and what you allow into your field. #frequencyhacking

To get a handle on how this works, I'd like you to consider the staggering range of potential life experiences that are available to every human being. In this single moment in time, some people are experiencing utter devastation, some are living over-the-top joy and exaltation, and others are having life experiences that fall at literally every point in between. Now that you understand the process of creation, you know that each of us generates our own experience of life based on the energetic frequency of the thoughts, moods, feelings, and actions we offer in every moment, and the respective frequencies of the people with whom we exchange energy in our interactions. And while we cannot dictate circumstances or control the behaviors of others, we always have control over how we choose to flow our own energy. I will repeat this again because it is so important: we always have control over how we choose to flow our own energy.

Write this down somewhere. Put it up on your bathroom mirror. I AM RESPONSIBLE FOR WHAT I CHOOSE TO INTERACT WITH AND HOW I DIRECT THE ENERGY THAT I AM. Where your attention goes, energy flows. This means that if someone treats you badly, you can choose to fester over that situation and use all your precious mental, emotional, and physical energy to internally spin yourself into a depleted heap. And you also have the ability to stop stewing about it, stop talking about it, and stop seeking the agreement of others about how terrible this person is.

To understand why the latter, and not the former, is the wisest choice, just think of it in terms of energy: if you manage to enroll ten friends or family members in the perspective that you were treated badly, you now have yourself and ten other people flowing energy into the negative situation; and with every thought and feeling directed that way, you are fueling, with the power of your own precious vital energy, the continuation of an unwanted experience. But if you stop flowing your energy toward that negative experience by omitting it from your thoughts, feelings, conversation, and attention, it will, over time, stop playing on your reality movie screen.

Your attention has the power to create experiences. In the same way that a radio tower broadcasts a whole range of frequencies into the airwaves, allowing you the freedom to choose which station to tune into, you also have the power to choose the frequency at which you live your life and the frequency of what you allow into your life. In other words, frequency is a choice.

Inspired Action

- Where do you need to begin frequency-hacking your life?

- What are you directing your energy towards that is not in alignment with the joy, peace, and happiness that you would like to be experiencing?

When you stop talking about it, stop thinking about it, and give it up to the Universe to handle instead, you reclaim your energy and release yourself from negative, cyclical patterns. Now, you are free to direct your energy towards the creation of your choice.

Frequency Exchange

I hope you're getting the sense by now that we are all walking, breathing frequency generators, taking on the energy of those around us and emitting energy of our own onto others. There is a constant symphony of energy exchange going on in every moment, and all of us are affected by the vibrations that are occurring around us. If you strike a C chord on a piano, every other resonant chord on the keyboard will vibrate in harmony with that note. And in the same way, human beings register vibrations, and experience either resonance or discord in response to interacting with others.

Both on unconscious levels and on purpose, we absorb and align with the:

- Energy
- Moods
- Tendencies
- Patterns
- Beliefs

...of the people and things we encounter. This is why—once we've reconnected with our soul frequency and have begun manifesting it in different aspects of our lives—it becomes vital that we create an environment around ourselves that encourages this energy to flourish. A young plant requires nourishment from the sun and protection from the wind in order to survive. So too our soul frequency must be guarded and cultivated in order to continue building momentum. Your newfound clarity is so precious, and your quest to live in alignment with your truest self is a vision that deserves to be nourished with support and love.

We all have a set point as to how much energy, abundance, and goodness we are accustomed to allowing into our lives.

Alignment, that all powerful 20%, supports us in transitioning from short-term gains into what I call "forever results." We all have a set point as to how much energy, abundance, and goodness we are accustomed to allowing into our lives. Many times when we make changes, we forget that maintaining those changes requires us to adjust our lifestyle to help us sustain that set point. Without structures in place that anchor this new energy into being, you may slip back into negative internal dialogue, familiar bad-feelings, and non-serving, self-sabotaging behaviors. Human beings are creatures of habit. Unless we make the deliberate choice to resonate with the frequency of our soul, we may find ourselves unconsciously falling into resonance with those around us.

At the most fundamental level, no one likes to make other people uncomfortable. Because we are social creatures, we naturally want to feel connected with those around us, to feel as though we understand them and are understood by them. But, if in the name of not overturning the applecart, we allow the tone of our frequency to be set according to other people's perceptions, beliefs, or choices, we put ourselves at risk of backsliding into attitudes and behaviors that will not bring us the results we desire. Maintaining alignment with your soul frequency is all about becoming acutely aware of your own energy so you can protect the new space you have found for yourself.

Protecting Your Creations

Like attracts like. We tend to resonate with people who reside at a similar frequency because it's both comfortable and non-threatening. So, when you're no longer transmitting on the channel that your family members or peers have been accustomed to finding you on, it's very likely that they will become uncomfortable and may even start to act out in some way. This can show up as teasing, making small -minded or intimidating remarks, taking passive-aggressive jabs when you demonstrate a new behavior, or withdrawing their energy from the relationship entirely. In some cases it may seem like those around you will stop at nothing to test your resolve or knock you off your game; but you have to understand that most of the time they are not doing this intentionally. They've just gotten comfortable with your old energy patterns and the change in your frequency feels threatening. At a subconscious level they are trying to bring you back to the vibe they're accustomed to feeling from you.

I have seen many women make incredible strides toward raising their frequency only to fall off the rails when those close to them react to these changes in a less-than-positive way. And I certainly understand this. When I first left my previous career to start my own business, many people just didn't get it. Since I had spent so much of my life up to that point navigating my choices according to someone else's compass, many people did not know the real me; and let's be real—to some degree, neither did I. They had no way to understand the evolution that was happening in my inner world because my inner reality was just that, internal, and was yet to be expressed in the outer world. I felt like I was living a double life in some ways.

When I started coming out of hiding, I could only imagine how confusing this new direction was to some people around me. "What are you doing with your life? Are you really going to give up a career you have invested fifteen years in?" Their confusion was justified; but at the time, it felt like a lack of understanding and support. And yet, for the first time in my life, I was not deterred. I knew I was right on track. I was listening to something much stronger and more resonant than anything I had ever experienced: those powerful whispers of the soul.

For the first time ever, I didn't let anybody hijack my energy. I used to allow people to weigh in on my ideas and proceed to tear them down before they had even gotten off the ground. Rather than protecting my fledgling creation, I would fall back into alignment with their opinions and perspectives. But this time, I didn't falter. I didn't give anyone that type of power over my creations. I just got stronger, and the reason I did is because I started to protect my energy.

Naysayers will slow our momentum down

if we let them, like throwing a ratchet into the spokes of our fast-spinning bicycle tire.

A new desire—to switch careers, to get your body back into shape, to leave a relationship, to find your purpose—has a lot of momentum behind it when it is freshly hatched. By listening to other people's opinions about why that might not be such a good idea or why we shouldn't be spending our time or money that way, we lose some of the initial momentum created by our excitement. Our job is to keep all our ducks in a row, if you will, by focusing our thoughts, emotions, and energy only in the direction of what we *do* want. To allow our attention to deviate even for a few minutes in an opposing direction is so harmful to that new creation because it splits our energy. Half of us is wanting it and half of us is doubting our ability to have it. Naysayers will slow our momentum down if we let them, like throwing a ratchet into the spokes of our fast-spinning bicycle tire.

How often do we invite people into our creative life, allow them to tear it apart, and then believe their harsh critiques over our own inner knowing?

If anyone made a single derogatory comment about my son, I would not entertain it for one moment. I would chalk up the comment as ridiculous and walk away from the fool who said it. I would never dream of allowing someone to insult my son, and I'd fight like a lioness with anyone who tried. As women we are fierce about protecting our offspring, but we don't defend our own creations with the same protectiveness—and we need to! How often do we invite people into our creative life, allow them to tear it apart and then believe their harsh critiques over our own inner knowing? This happens daily in the lives of far too many women—whether it's in response to a new clothing style we're trying on for size, a change in our career aspirations, an idea for a new invention, the way we parent, or how we choose to spend our time. We put ourselves up on the chopping block on the daily and withstand the blows of the opinionated as we watch the things we love and are passionate about wilt and shrivel up. This had certainly been my experience in the past; but it wasn't going to happen ever again.

By this point in my transformation, I understood energy, and I protected the energy of my new creations by limiting my exposure to anyone or anything that wasn't aligned with the direction I was headed. Now, this might seem harsh, but when you understand the power of energy, you understand that for anything in its infant stage to grow into maturity, it must be coddled, tended to and shielded from any adverse force. Because the beginning stage of its life is where the most important growth happens. In the presence of your love and focus, your vision will grow into something big and strong, eventually able to withstand adversity; but first it needs to be watered daily and be well taken care of. In the absence of your loving attention and scorched by the hot rays of criticism, it will fizzle out.

That is the impact of not protecting your energy. People go without what they need, and you go without the soul-gratifying experience of fulfilling those needs.

Here's a valuable perspective that may help you understand the importance of protecting your creations: imagine for a moment that you fulfilling your vision will result in your product, service, or contribution to humanity, helping a hundred thousand or more people to improve some area of their lives. If you did not protect your energy at the very beginning stages of that vision—if you permitted the naysayers to diminish it with skepticism and doubt—those hundred thousand or more people would go without your help. That is the impact of you not being *you* in the world. That is the impact of not protecting your energy. People go without what they need, and you go without the gratifying experience of fulfilling those needs. The contribution you are here to make is unique only to you. No one else has your perspective, and no one else can serve in the same way that you can. You are special, and when you realize that in the depths of your being, you will understand how vital it is to protect the gift that you are.

You are special,
and when you realize that in the depths of your being, you will understand how vital it is to protect the gift that you are.

I get it. It can be really tough to hold your frequency high when others are doing all kinds of things to engage you in old behaviors that make themselves feel more secure. In my private practice, I explain this potential downfall to all of my clients and encourage them to keep an eye out for it before it subtly or not so subtly derails them from their intentions. I also coach them in a technique I've developed to resolve frequency gap issues within relationships. Basically, the technique is to withdraw one's attention from the discordant aspects of life so as not to give them power, and to go about the business of practicing our new, higher frequency habits.

So what to do if your increased vibrancy or spiritual growth triggers insecurity in someone close to you and they say or do something to diminish your light? Well, simply being aware that their reaction is not intended to hurt you will help to provide some healthy psychological distance. Their seemingly personal attacks are not personal, although they feel entirely personal. It is simply a sub-conscious attempt to try to bring your frequency back down to where others feel more comfortable, and to tempt you to realign your energy back into resonance with theirs. You have to steer clear of the drama. It is so important, because typically people take these kinds of jabs in order to get you emotionally engaged so you'll jab back—and in so doing, lower your frequency. But once you are aware of this tendency, you no longer have to interact with it. You can make the choice to hold your frequency high even when you're met with resistance from others.

If you can avoid the temptation to return fire and are able to maintain your alignment, one of two things is likely to happen in each of your close relationships.

- In the first scenario, the person may eventually realize that their passive-aggressive comments aren't succeeding in getting you to lower your frequency to meet theirs and may decide to raise *their* frequency to achieve resonance with you again. Perhaps they'll become curious about the changes you're making and say something to the effect of, "So, tell me again why eating that kale soup helps?" or "Maybe I should try some of that too." Like a moth to a flame, those who are ready to embody more of their truth will be drawn to you expressing yours. Instead of trying to drag you down, they'll seek to bring themselves up to where your frequency is. Partnerships of every kind take a wonderful and fresh new turn when this occurs, because both of you can continue to grow together, reinventing your relationship again and again, reinforcing higher frequencies in one another, and expanding both as individuals and in unison.

- The other scenario you may encounter when seeking to maintain alignment with your soul frequency, is that some friends and family members may become increasingly uncomfortable with who you now are and will start to distance themselves from you in some way. They may say things like, "Who are you trying to be?" or "I am not sure we see eye to eye anymore." Again, it's important to realize that this is not personal. It's simply an indication that the gap in your frequencies is too wide. The mismatch causes a sensation that is registered by them as discomfort; and to protect *their* energy frequency, they pull away.

If this occurs, you must realize that it's just as beautiful an unfolding as someone who decides they want to raise their energy along with you. Remember, you are recreating your life from the inside out in a state of resonance and alignment, and if people are not in alignment within themselves, their energy is not going to resonate with you. You may still feel love for those people, but you will not feel much commonality. It will also be hard for them to support something in you that they are not supporting and following within themselves. Being in their presence is not going to feel good to you anymore, in the same way your energy doesn't feel altogether comfortable to them.

Allowing

It requires some deep breaths, patience, and willpower in order to allow things to be as they are. We all have a deep desire to fix things. We desperately want to feel comfortable and to make others comfortable, often to the point that we will pretzel ourselves into a twisted, self-sacrificing mess to avoid feelings of discomfort. This tendency is especially common in intimate relationships, where we naturally strive to stay on the same page as our partners. But the discomfort you feel when you interact with a loved one after you've experienced growth in some aspect of life is an important initiation into a new frequency. Instead of trying to eradicate it at all costs, I encourage you to simply allow the discomfort to be there. See if you can just be with it, and let it wash over you like a gentle wave. Allow yourself to feel it fully and you may find that it will start to dissipate and resolve itself, either through the natural actions you take on your behalf or through actions that others take on theirs.

Now, here's the kicker about all of this frequency raising you are doing. You are going to see things about your life and people in it that you have never seen before. The first reaction is usually to not believe it. You must remember that the truth rises, and as you connect to yours, you will start to see the deepest inner truths of others, sometimes by sensing it and other times by new people showing it to you. Seeing and feeling these truths requires allowing. They may be joyous, but they can also be hurtful. You must allow the Universe to reveal these truths to you and remain open to the new perspectives that you will be shown.

You are going to see things about your life and people in it that you have never seen before. The first reaction is usually to not believe it.

We all have a deep desire to know what is going to happen, to achieve a final result or get to a final destination. We're uncomfortable with the in-between spaces and allowing growth to occur at its own pace and in its right time. It is often challenging to allow the truths to be revealed to us and to feel those truths fully, and yet that is exactly how we stay connected to our soul frequency.

To continually reconnect with the resounding truth inside of us means allowing people to reveal their true nature and allowing circumstances to evolve enough so that we can get a feel for how we want to interact with them—and both of these things require a generous amount of time and space.

Inspired Action

Have you ever had someone offer to help you or to take you to dinner and it just didn't feel right to you? Me too. My advice going forward is that if ever you feel like there is an ulterior motive behind someone's behavior, or that their intentions are not on par with yours, *allow* yourself to take a moment before you feel pressured to say yes. Allow yourself to really explore the feelings going on inside of you, and to ask yourself if this is the right fit at the right time. Allow yourself to discover your inner truth about this person and give yourself the space and the permission to communicate the right choice for you in your own time.

Allowing is taking a breath, a pause, a moment of introspection, to reconnect with your soul frequency. The act of allowing paves the road to discernment and clarity in all relationships, decisions, and forward motion. Allow things to be, allow yourself to feel, allow yourself to be truthful, and you'll find that it becomes increasingly easier to adjust the groove as needed.

Adjusting the Groove

Sometimes we're compelled to choose certain people and things not because they feel good in the moment, but simply because they are the choices we've historically made. The truth is, life is unfolding fresh and new in every moment. Yet, over time, human beings develop a strong tendency to think and feel and do the same things, over and over, day after day, out of habit. Soon a well-worn groove is carved into the brain's neural pathways, and it takes both sensitivity and intention to make sure we aren't just blindly rolling down a dead-end road.

Let's say, for the sake of example, that you've been in the habit of going to lunch with your three best pals at work—all of whom eat fast food—and you have recently decided to become a salad-loving gal. In the first few days, weeks, or months following your decision, you may have no problem joining your friends at the burger place and eating the salad you brought from home. But eventually you may notice yourself pecking a few of their French fries, then a bite of a burger, and maybe even moving on to ordering a whole fast food meal for yourself, chalking it up to a "splurge" day. Once choices like these are set into motion, they gain more and more momentum. Soon you start craving that kind of food again and little by little the unwanted frequency—and, on its heels, the unwanted experience—is once again a primary part of your life, without you even realizing that you invited it in.

And now suppose, for example, that you made the choice to dine with three different people who had all come to their own personal decisions around desiring to eat in a healthy manner. Can you see how much easier it would be to stay on the same page with them—and with your intention? In fact, at a certain point, it would become almost effortless. The strength of your collective commitment would inspire you to support one another in extremely creative ways—maybe by taking turns prepping a big salad to be shared by all, or by exchanging healthy dressing recipes, to name just a few possibilities.

You simply wouldn't be called to eat fast food with these friends. Who they are as people and the choices they are making serve as a powerful support system and structure that make it easy for you to remain at a high frequency—simply by virtue of who they are *being* in the world. What you consistently hang around, you eventually become. This is the sentiment conveyed in the Spanish phrase, "Tell me who you walk with and I will tell you who you are," which translates in English as the ever-familiar, "Birds of a feather flock together." This is true on a physical level, and even deeper, on an energetic level.

If you want to live beyond what others think is possible, invite people into your life who are already living that way and begin to connect with their energy.

If you want to live beyond what others think is possible, invite people into your life who are already living that way and begin to connect with their energy. I have seen both in my own experience and from helping so many people activate their soul frequency, that if you change the people you spend most of your time with, you will change the trajectory of your life. You can't join yourself at the hip to low-frequency people and expect to live a high frequency life. A natural byproduct of being around inspiring people is that without even trying, you become more inspired.

You can't join yourself at the hip to low-frequency people and expect to live a high frequency life. A natural byproduct of being around inspiring people is that without even trying, you become more inspired.

Unless we make a conscious declaration about who we are going to be, how we are going to show up, and what choices we are committed to making in each situation we encounter, it's very likely that we'll harmonize with whatever frequency is the most dominant. Often this is synonymous to sinking to the lowest common denominator. The more you understand energy, the more you'll begin to notice that in every interaction, there is a subtle dance going on behind the scenes that plays out in all kinds of ways as each person unconsciously tries to dominate the vibration and get others to climb aboard their energy bandwagon. And the thing to understand is that energy never stands still, which means that you are always moving in one direction or another.

Many of the power struggles that occur in intimate relationships are caused by trying to find resonance in spite of a large gap in frequencies. One person wants the other person to ride on their energy wave and vice versa. Life is much smoother when we connect with people at a similar resonance. It feels more peaceful, and it's much easier to understand each other. Oftentimes, when we find ourselves in relationships and situations that are grossly out of alignment, it is because we didn't allow ourselves the space to really listen for our truth before jumping in with both feet. Once we learn that we really can trust that little voice inside that urges us when something is or isn't right, we can begin to head these situations off at the pass and save ourselves a lot of strife.

Trust Yourself

When we first start working together, many women share that they feel unclear about the next step to take in some important area of their lives and are anguishing over what is the "right" decision. Often, this confusion is simply the result of years of going against one's own inner compass, of rolling over it, or pretending not to have received its guidance when the information it provides might cause messiness or inconvenience. It's like taking a bat to the smoke alarm in your home before checking to see if there's a fire. Sure, the high-pitched squeal is silenced for now; but eventually, ignoring the message will burn down the house. Life is noisy, and if you want to hear your soul speaking, you need to get quiet. Before you become intimate with the tone and frequency of your own inner voice and the methods it uses to direct your attention, it can be very easy to dismiss or ignore it.

Each time we forsake our intuition in the name of something or someone outside of ourselves, we close off the once wide-open connection with our own soul urgings that we were all born to experience, and we slowly begin to fragment our life. Without a solid rapport with our own inner compass—which alerts us to the moment by moment ebb and flow of our needs, passions, and desires—we build up resentment and resignation that slowly drains the sparkle from our eyes.

A woman's trust in herself goes through the roof when she learns to listen to the subtle whispers that come from within. And just so you know, these communications do not always sound like harps and angels, nor are they always deep or profound. Your soul is passionately interested in every aspect of your human life and is always available to guide you—in big decisions as well as in the minutia we all encounter day-to-day, like which route to take on the drive home, which gift to buy your best friend, and whether you want to serve sandwiches or wraps for your next luncheon. We have got to evolve into trusting the knowing that bubbles up from deep within, so we can move forward in faith when we are asked to close the door on certain aspects of our lives—even when we have no idea what may be waiting behind the door that lies ahead. The more practiced you become in trusting your own compass, the more confidently you'll be able to distinguish the clear whisper of your soul from the convoluted voice of fear. Eventually, the signal you'll pick up most easily will be the one being transmitted by your soul frequency, while that other chaotic radio station fades far into the distance.

The more practiced you become in trusting your own compass, the more confidently you'll be able to distinguish the clear whisper of your soul from the convoluted voice of fear.

There is perhaps no higher feeling of empowerment available to us as women (or men, for that matter) than to receive an impulse from within, to follow it even though it's urging us in an uncharted direction, to be led to an even better outcome than we could have possibly imagined, and then to stand in full realization of our own brilliance.

Wow, just wow!

It's a feeling of invincibility, of ultimate worthiness, of being unstoppable. And best of all, this feeling is completely sustainable because you generated it from within. It's never that others were standing in your way; it's that you have been in your own way because you've been seeing life through a lens of limitation and lack, and now you're free because you've taken off those glasses. Once you come to know that you truly can trust yourself, you'll move forward with certainty, secure in the knowledge that the whisper of your soul will never lead you astray.

Course Correction

You know that feeling you get when you absent-mindedly take a wrong turn on your way to an important appointment and you are running late? Panic is often our kneejerk reaction when we realize we've fallen off track. Oftentimes a woman will come to our weekly coaching sessions so upset about falling out of alignment with her commitment to healthier eating, creating a change in her business, or losing sight of an intention she's set in some other key area of her life. What's really interesting is that the way she handles the experience of falling off track has *everything* to do with how quickly she'll get back in the flow.

Some people experience getting off track as if it is constantly happening, and view getting back on track as very difficult. This is reflected in their language, which usually sounds something like, "I always blow it," "I never meet my goals," etc. The thing to realize is that falling off track is only falling out of alignment with our own inner compass—and that because its guidance is constant and steady, we always have a clear shot back home.

The first part of mastering the art of course correction is to realize that you were never really on course to begin with.

The first part of mastering the art of course correction is to realize that you were never really on course to begin with. Navigating a soul-inspired life is more like steering a boat than driving along a well-traveled road. If you've ever driven a boat then you know that the boat never goes straight. It's always course correcting– a little bit left, a little bit right, a little bit left, a little bit right– and the closer you stay to the center, closest to going straight, the faster the boat gets to its destination. This understanding may help you let yourself off the hook and find some peace in the fact that you are never heading exactly straight ahead. Feeling a little movement and flexibility in this fact? I hope so, because it's only our resistance to what is and our criticism of ourselves that introduce stress into any equation.

To understand how exactly this is so, let's say you are on a boat headed toward one of your important goals. The goal might relate to food, health, weight, relationships, career, living space, or really anything or anyone in your life. But for whatever reason, in relation to this subject, instead of making minor, moment by moment adjustments when your inner compass urges you to course correct, you are playing the "Oh no, I've gotten off track. Not *again*!" game. Something happens that makes you aware that you are not where you want to be in this aspect of life, and panic or frustration sets in. Determined, you commit to getting back on track, so you grab the wheel of the boat and crank it all the way to the right because you so desperately want to get away from where you are now. This is what I affectionately call the "I need to lose ten pounds by next week so I am going to drink only juices and water" syndrome. Not the most eloquent phrase, but I think you get my drift.

When we stop **zigzagging** across the ocean, wasting gas and getting nowhere, we have so much more energy to enjoy life and more attention to devote to maintaining a consistent course to our desired destination.

Driven by sheer willpower, you keep turning your proverbial boat all the way to the right for a few weeks, full power ahead, until finally you are exhausted from bumping around in the waves and being tousled by the headwinds, and you just can't go another inch. In desperate need of a respite, you pull the wheel all the way left and go full speed ahead in the opposite direction. This is the moment when, after having done so "good" at "not really eating anything" for a week, you spy the buffet at the weekend brunch joint and then all bets are off. With this approach, you are basically being tossed around in a raging sea, over-correcting in all directions in an attempt to find some figment of balance or control.

If instead of becoming more determined, we focused on becoming more practiced in the art of course correcting at earlier, subtle stages—when the message our inner compass delivers is just an inkling—we would save ourselves a whole lot of heartache and headache with regard to weight and health, relationships and business. When we stop zigzagging across the ocean, wasting gas and getting nowhere, we have so much more energy to enjoy life and more attention to devote to maintaining a consistent course to our desired destination. It is important to get comfortable with small corrections instead of sweeping movements from right to left so you can use your energy in the manner that is most effective to get you where you want to go.

I see so many women who've arrived at the midpoint of their lives feeling exhausted, overwhelmed and utterly spent. The inefficient use of their energy—coupled with the discord created by following someone else's map rather than the one they were born with—has depleted them. The constant forward motion in one direction followed by over-compensating in another has split their energy and weakened their life force and they feel they have nothing left for themselves—not even a moment alone to just BE.

Inspired Action

- Where do you feel the need to course correct?

- What do you habitually do that depletes you rather than recharges you?

- It's time to bring your lifestyle into greater alignment with your soul by reviewing, restructuring, and recreating your day-to-day routine.

- What responsibilities can you turn over to someone else? Be creative!

- Where do you need to ask for help? It matters, and your happiness is important!

Cringe-Worthy

It's an ugly truth that no one wants to admit; but most women are downright terrified of being judged by other women, whether we experience their judgment in overt ways, such as gossiping about friends, or in covert, passive-aggressive ways, such as the silent but dreaded disapproving look. After sitting with hundreds of women, I have heard story after story of women feeling judged by their mothers, sisters, friends, acquaintances, co-workers, and even perfect strangers passing them on the street. In case the prospect of being judged by others makes you cringe, let me cut straight to the chase. In the process of creating what you truly want in your life, you *are* going to be judged, possibly shamed, and likely rejected by some, and what I am about to share with you will probably make you cringe: you are going to have to put yourself first in your life in order not to succumb to pressure from those around you who would much prefer you to put *them* first.

As women, we are taught that the mark of successful womanhood is to always put the needs of our partners, families, friends, and especially our children ahead of our own—and to not only put them first, but to do so at the expense of taking proper care of ourselves, mentally, physically, emotionally, and even financially. When I suggest that my clients put themselves first, the word S-E-L-F-I-S-H is usually the first thing to flash across their minds. Prioritizing your needs first is *not* being selfish; but because we are accustomed to considering our lives through a black-and-white lens, we have come to believe that we are either self-sacrificing or we are selfish. This is a mindset that simply must be transformed if you are going to let yourself shine.

> *Prioritizing your needs first* is not being selfish, but because we are accustomed to considering our lives through a black-and-white lens, we have come to believe that we are either self-sacrificing or we are selfish.

Putting yourself first means caring for your wellbeing first, not instead of or at the expense of others. It means you take the fifteen minutes to enjoy a hot shower. You leave your office to take a walk outside for thirty minutes to breathe and just BE. You give yourself an hour to ponder the new idea that's been percolating within you, before you head off to start your day. You invest in your ideas. You buy yourself a new outfit that will make you feel your best for a Friday night out on the town. You let people help you with your kids so you can get your nails done. You take a dance class on Wednesday nights because you love it. And fueling all of these self-care actions and any others that float your boat is your belief that YOU ARE WORTHY OF YOUR OWN TIME, MONEY, AND LOVE, and you are not afraid to own that when a pack of ladies who don't believe in their own worthiness try to shame you for living the life you were born to live.

We cannot be great for others if we're not first great for ourselves. Giving away your energy when you are running on empty doesn't make you a heroine; it makes you resentful, discontent, devoid of vibrant energy, and disconnected from your own inner compass—and quite frankly, not that much fun to be around.

Giving away your energy when you are running on empty doesn't make you a heroine; it makes you resentful, discontent, devoid of vibrant energy, and disconnected from your own inner compass—and quite frankly, not that much fun to be around.

The only person who has the power to make sure you fill your own cup is YOU. You cannot wait for anyone to step up and give you permission to take great care of yourself, and you will for sure not find this encouragement from those who are not yet committed students of the art of self-care. The faster you surround yourself with people who support you in loving yourself big time, the better your life is going to get, the more you are going to be able to create, and the faster your evolution is going to be. Please know that I, for one, give you full permission to take the time and space you need to take impeccable care of your most valuable asset: yourself.

Inspired Action

- What are three things that you can do for yourself each week to give back to YOU?

- Is it taking a long bath, getting your nails done, taking a run, meditating, going to the gym, getting a facial, or carving out a little time to read a book uninterrupted?

Whatever it is for you, schedule those three things first on your calendar, as they are the most important part of your week. When you are committed to self-care and give generously to yourself, everything and everyone in your life benefits!

The Big Give

The difference between a person who is a master at something and the person who is not yet, lies in how that person shows up for the task at hand each day. Just because you have done something every day for twenty years doesn't mean you are a master. And just because you just started doing something a year ago does not mean you can't become a master. A singer can show up and perform a song, or she can move an audience to tears with her power, passion, and the life force she communicates through the music. A mother can make sure her children are fed and clothed, or she can go beyond that by looking them in the eye, getting on the floor, playing, and listening to their heart's desires. A business owner can keep the company in the black, but she can also go the extra mile by treating each person who walks in the door like gold.

In this world, there are many takers, some givers, and even fewer people who consistently give big from the heart; but the latter group is easy to recognize. They're the ones who still step on the stage with the same excitement they had when they got their big break years ago. We all know that "phoning it in" is easy. The Big Give is going all the way. It is in the details, in the moments you create for another person that impact them in a way that they never forget. When you give big, you emit a powerful energy that everyone who crosses your path can feel. The Big Give is the very definition of generosity and the opposite of self-sacrifice. Letting other people take from you or extending yourself beyond what is healthy will only lead you down the road to burnout. Being able to give at the level I'm talking about is only possible when your cup is full. And because it comes from fullness, it's self-replenishing.

Being able to give at the level I'm talking about is only possible when your cup is full. And because it comes from fullness, it's self-replenishing.

Giving nourishes the soul of the giver like nothing else does. The exchange of energy is so pure. You give big and seeing the impact on others fills you with pure joy. This is a complete energy exchange where both people are made better from the experience. When we are in Big Give mode, any self-doubt, self-judgment, or fear gives way to the feeling of high frequency energy flowing through your actions. We can't be tearing ourselves down while focusing on giving big to another. Those two states of being can't coexist. If you ever find yourself in a funk, go give your beautiful, precious, and unique energy to another so fully that your ego dissolves in the experience as you become one with the energy of giving. As Pablo Picasso said, "The meaning of life is to find your gift; the purpose of life is to give it away." Sharing the gifts that you are here to contribute does more than lighten your mood; it illumines the path to a higher way of living.

Inspired Action

- When your cup is full, what do you naturally feel compelled to share?
- What is the special something inside of you that can help others? Own your gifts!
- Write down whatever comes to mind first and start giving big.

Finding Your Tribe

When you're surrounded by people who do not understand—or, at the very least, respect the new direction of your life or the importance of taking great care of self, it's very easy to get discouraged in their presence. Those who are still drowning out the whispers of their own inner voice simply cannot understand why you are so intent on following yours. And people who are not living their purpose have no ability to support you in doing so. As we have explored, it's important to say "no" to the negative energy that some folks bring into your life and to become aware when something in a relationship no longer feels right. Both of these actions will protect your new creations from influences that may steer them sideways. But for your vision to take off in a really big way, you need to find people you can share it with who understand it enough to become true champions of your cause.

Finding your tribe isn't just about networking or making some new acquaintances. It's purposefully connecting with those who are conscious enough to support your highest expression, people who see you and "get" you and can metaphorically (and sometimes literally) hold your hand as you take the steps your soul calls you to take. In the presence of people who understand the power of energy and are committed to keeping their own vibration high, your intentions will be magnified and your forward motion will increase tenfold. From these associations, you'll find inspiration, new ideas, and resources; and a valuable source of support and feedback.

As I began drawing new and wonderful people into my experience, there was no doubt in my mind that they had come with a purpose. Each meeting was rich in synchronicities, and there was an undeniable recognition in our eyes. The more comfortable I became with honoring and following the whispers of my soul, and sharing with others the wisdom that had led me to a deeper understanding of myself, the more people showed up in my life who were on a similar path. I was attracting people in a similar resonance to my own. It was as if we could almost talk to each other without speaking.

You will know
when you find your tribe.
You will feel it, see it, and
know it deep in your heart.
Finding your tribe feels like
coming home.

Since those early days, my tribe has continued to widen and deepen, and I truly would not be who I am or where I am today without the contribution of the many beautiful souls who have stepped into my life. Sometimes, I am in utter awe of this life and the people I get to share it with. I am amazed at the variety of avenues they came through and the synchronistic, so-called "chance" meetings. I share this to encourage you to trust that when you encounter others who stir in you a vague sense of recognition, or with whom you feel an instant sense of comfort or ease, to trust this feeling and follow its lead, for it's very likely that your connection with this person is much bigger than only this lifetime. You will know when you find your tribe. You will feel it, see it, and know it deep in your heart. Finding your tribe feels like coming home.

As you continue to embody your soul frequency, you will find that some members of your soul family roll into your experience effortlessly and spontaneously—for example, a friend introduces you to someone and you feel like you have known this person forever. Or you happen to notice the woman sitting next to you at the local coffee shop is reading the very book that someone just recommended. And if you notice and appreciate the unplanned yet synchronistic encounters that start happening all around you, you will start increasing your chances of drawing even more new soul friends into your life.

What distinguishes this person as a part of your soul family is that they are someone you can learn from, someone who will broaden your perspective as you take a peek at life through their eyes. Some will be friends with whom you love to sit and ponder the universe and all its intricate perfection, while others may challenge you and spur you powerfully into action.

The common denominator you are looking for is inspiration. What about this person inspires you? What can you learn from them and them from you? What seeds of wisdom do they have to share? The truth is, the world around you is teeming with living, breathing examples of every possible experience that you desire to create. If you desire peace, sit with someone who embodies peace. If you want to start a business, share tea with someone who owns a successful business. Tune your frequency to them and become open to receive their gifts and share yours. At any moment you have the ability to welcome and call in souls who infuse positive energy into your life.

Next time you walk into a new situation, take an inventory of the people in the environment. As your brain sorts information such as noticing who is there, what they are wearing, and how they are behaving, go deeper. Feel out the room on an energetic level and notice where there is resonance between you and others. When you have a soul connection, you will feel compelled to engage. Even if your logical mind tells you the two of you have nothing in common, some part of you will sense that there is an exchange of energy that wants to take place between you, and that your highest good will be served if you allow this exchange to take place.

Whenever you catch yourself thinking or saying things like, "She was really cool," or "That place had a great vibe," I want you to stop and really pay attention. This is a sign, a clue, and a whisper from the universe that is urging you to take a few more steps in a particular direction. The 'vibe' you felt means you liked a particular frequency—not because it's universally likeable, but because it resonated with you. The phenomenon we call attraction is nothing more than when our energetic soul frequency is vibrating within a similar range to something or someone else. This is how relationships of all types are formed.

Your tribe is truly a soul family. Understanding flows easily in all directions, and there is a free exchange of energy and ideas between you. You are like members of the same team, supporting one another toward your individual and collective goals, and taking one another higher at every turn. In the company of high-minded others, your energy is liberated from the obligation of "getting through" stale social situations and you are free to experience life in a much lighter and brighter way. You'll no longer feel compelled to force yourself to attend an event you dread going to for the sake of people-pleasing, and you'll no longer have the energy or the tolerance to deny the things that really do call to you and captivate your genuine interest. Maybe you're an artist who was born into a family of scientists? If so, you can be sure that in the presence of others who are passionately creating art, that long lost part of you will once again come alive. The members of your tribe often serve as catalysts that make it easier for you to reclaim aspects of yourself that you left behind in childhood.

Your soul is encoded with everything you need to live the life that you most want to live. Your soul family will show you the way home to you. They will lift you up when you need it, challenge you when you get stuck, and hold you to your greatness. These are some of the life-giving, mind-expanding benefits that come from having a supportive community; but I can tell you from first-hand experience that the absolute coolest gift of finding your tribe is that you may—and maybe for the first time in years—begin to give yourself permission to be authentically and transparently who you are. And nothing feels better than that.

One of the biggest internal changes that happened for me is the level at which I felt comfortable being authentic with others, even with people I had never met. Long gone was the unconscious programming I'd been dragging around since childhood that told me it's not okay to reveal parts of myself that might not appear perfect or acceptable to others. I began to share myself more in every single way; and over time, I found that I cared less and less about what people thought about what I shared. Information was seeking expression through me around every corner and it became impossible not to allow it to flow.

When we can be authentic and really share ourselves with people, we open up to receiving more of their love, and we also give other people permission to be open and real about themselves and their lives. Only when we share from the depth of our hearts can we actually make a real connection, and this creates a ripple effect of authenticity. Transformation calls you up and your soul family will make sure you heed the call. We each have the power to inspire others to be more courageous, and this is how positive change, openness, transparency, and authenticity spread far and wide. Living this life to the fullest means you have to be willing to buck the current of the status quo and believe in yourself enough to chart your own course.

Be a Rebel

Conformity is the death of creative expression. Think about some of the most interesting, creative, and soulful people in the world of art and music. Names like David Bowie,

Lady GaGa, Prince, Cher, Madonna, Banksy, Frida Kahlo, Jackson Pollock, and certainly Picasso. What do these amazing artists have in common? They colored outside the lines. They had the courage to keep creating in the face of other people's opposition. We admire them because of their commitment to rebel from the status quo and to make manifest the vision that lived inside of them. These artists are respected for their courage and visions; but in the beginning, practically no one else got it. They faced criticism and pressure to conform, and this only made them stronger in their convictions. You may not agree with the cause they stood for, and you may hate their art, and yet you know them all the same. Their commitment to their own self-expression was so firm that they have become part of the fabric of our culture that will endure long after their own lifespan.

The best way to get people to stop raining on your parade is to help wake them up to what lives inside of them so they can join in the celebration and start directing their energy in more constructive and empowering ways.

You may not strive to be known on this same scale, and you may have no desire to create music or art; but there is something inside of you that wants to be expressed, and to give it life, you will have to become willing to be a bit of a rebel. Not everyone will get it. My advice is to hang out with those who do. The best way to get people to stop raining on your parade is to help wake them up to what lives inside of them so they can join in the celebration and start directing their energy in more constructive and empowering ways. To be a rebel is to do what came natural to you before people told you how to be. Nature just *is*, and being natural means we allow ourselves to just be.

My Grandma Dorothy was both a natural woman and a rebel, and she certainly saw the rebel in me. She deeply understood my heart and all its nuances. I remember as a child, staying the night at her house and every night before bed we would recite the 23 Psalm (her favorite) and the Christopher Robin prayers by heart. To this day I can still recall these at a moment's notice. My Grandma Dorothy was a deeply spiritual woman. She was a poet from the time she was a child, and a woman who definitely did things her own way.

Dorothy believed in me

without reservation and
she wanted more for me
than I ever dreamed possible
for myself.

Dorothy believed in me without reservation and she wanted more for me than I ever dreamed possible for myself. As I got older, she shared her love of crystals with me. She spoke about the afterlife. She told me stories of her father who was a hands-on healer, musician, and the inventor of one of the very first hearing aids. Dorothy was a beatnik in the '20s, and made the choice to divorce an abusive husband at a time when divorce was still the mark of shame. Even though she came from a family with status and wealth, she married my grandfather for love and enjoyed fifty-three happy and caring years of marriage with her husband until he passed. She was a renegade long before it was popular or even acceptable for women to break out of the societal norms. She was very aware that there was life beyond her human experience and I could talk to her for hours about things that no one else understood. She saved me in so many ways, validated who I was, and reminded me to always shoot for the stars. To the beautiful, eternal energy that was once manifested as Dorothy, I am forever grateful.

Sometimes we encounter only one Grandma Dorothy in the course of our lives. One person who gets it, who gets you, and isn't afraid to question and expand the boundaries in life. One person who stands for you, who thinks your quirks or geekiness are streaks of genius and always finds ways to lift you up, make you feel special, and assure you that everything that you are is great and everything you want in life is possible.

I now have the great honor and opportunity of awakening the rebel in the lives of other women as they make their way out of the darkness of disconnection, into their inner strength and innate capabilities. I shine a light on their path in the same way my grandmother did for me. It is a role that I don't take lightly. My hope is that every woman has a rebel in her life who gives her the space to express her truth even when it's inconvenient, someone who believes in her enough for two, until she believes in herself.

I now have the great honor and opportunity of awakening the rebel in the lives of other women as they make their way out of the darkness of disconnection, into their inner strength and innate capabilities.

I Hear You

It only takes one person to hear your heart, see your intentions, and affirm your value for you to start believing in the beauty of who and what you are. It is in the listening of those around you that you are inspired to bloom into a beautiful flower. And I want you to know, even if we never meet on this plane of consciousness, that I see you. I support you. I get it. You've got this. Let these powerful phrases ignite the flame of truth inside of you to burn even brighter. To be heard is powerful. To be the listener is magical. Listening—*really listening*—changes everything. In a world of noise that drowns out certainty, it only takes one powerful listener to change the course of life for another human being.

In a world of noise
that drowns out certainty,
it only takes one powerful
listener to change the
course of life for another
human being.

The listening my grandmother had for me was profound. It changed the course of my life. Sometimes we think we need to shape the lives of children or grandchildren, that we need to manipulate outcomes and steer them in certain well-established directions, when what we really need to do is to listen to them and hear what they want for *themselves,* make room for *their* brilliance. In the space of your listening, ideas flourish and potential blossoms. Take out the earplugs of distraction and dissolve your own ego and aspirations for a moment to really listen to another person. Through the listening and understanding my grandmother had for me, I knew that at least one person understood me. Really, she was all I needed to keep moving forward in faith and with trust.

Listening from a place of awareness is an art and one that is worth learning and passing on to others. You never know whom in your life needs to be heard, and if it is you that needs someone to powerfully listen, I invite you to join me in the possibility that your own version of Grandma Dorothy is right now waiting for an opportunity to cross your path and say to you—with or without words—"I hear you." Being listened to and really understood by another may be the one thing that releases you from the past pain of not being heard and gives you the freedom to cross the threshold into acting, speaking, and thinking as you want, without holding back.

Inspired Action

- Who really listens to you?
- Who gets the real you? The parts you rarely share.
- Who sees more for your life than you do?
- Who is unafraid of your growth?
- Powerful champions in your life are priceless! Seek them out!

Freedom

The freedom to live in alignment with our own rhythms and preferences, and the freedom to spend our time in the manner we choose, is the experience that most people desire more than all other things combined. Some believe that freedom is something that must be earned; others feel like it is reserved for a select few. But freedom is not something to gain. It is the truth of who we are. Freedom is what is present when you have faced your fears, traversed through them, and come out the other side realizing that you are only ever where you are as a result of your beliefs. If you want to live free, you can at any moment begin to define that freedom for yourself. You can create it by releasing from anything that is covering up your true nature. It is only the mind that creates cages for us, binds us to outdated ideals, and stops us from experiencing our own true nature. One of the fastest ways to start experiencing your innate freedom is through transparency, which is simply the act of giving yourself the freedom to be who and what you truly are.

It is only the mind that creates cages for us, binds us to outdated ideals and stops us from experiencing our own true nature.

A tiger doesn't try to hide the fact that it is a predator. An elephant doesn't play small, and an eagle doesn't worry about being seen eating a fish. Nature shows its true colors and this is what makes it so beautiful. No one wants to see a bird trying to be a fish, or a horse acting like a coyote. Pretense distorts the eclectic beauty and the important balance inherent in all of nature, and this includes you. You have got to be you—authentic, free, unapologetic of who you are, and willing to belt it to the back row.

Sharing yourself transparently is one of the quickest ways to dissolve the fear of what other people may think. Once you break free of that, you gain access to so many more options and you have the courage to try them on because you couldn't care less what others are going to say or do in response. You are the tiger. No apology necessary for your fierce nature. Transparency gives you the freedom to own all of the aspects of self and find love for all the many facets of your personality.

Love

In the end, love is all that really matters. Really, the only reason we do anything in life is to feel the energy of love. It is a very high frequency to live on, and the most powerful healer of our mind, body, and spirit. The love you share with others begins with the love you cultivate within. Sometimes, you may access love through a walk in nature, painting, reading, a warm bath, or by staring up at the stars on a clear night. The truth is that you *are* love and everyone you encounter—no matter how insecure, nasty, passive-aggressive, or difficult they appear on the surface—is also love. Now, this understanding doesn't mean you have to put up with terrible behavior (please don't), but it will allow you to see that underneath all misdirected methods a person may be using is the desire to be loved.

When you have had the opportunity to spend time with many people in a close and intimate way, as I have, you begin to see that if you reduce down to the common denominator in every interaction of human life, you always get to love. Why is the mother at the grocery store so nasty to her child? It is possibly because she was never shown the love *she* needed as a child. Her primary caregivers, the ones designed to love her most and provide her a sense of security, were rude and harsh to her, so she replicates this: to love her own child is to be combative. Similarly, the little boy at school acting out for attention is desperately seeking love. The irritable man at the gas station has lived alone without a hug for twenty-five years and his heart has become hardened from a lack of love. The difficult boss who is unsure that anything he does is good enough, is so demanding because he never received praise as a child and so he drives a hard line in hopes of finally earning the praise he so desperately needs.

We need love to survive like we need air and water and yet, we often have dysfunctional ways of expressing this need. When you understand that every human being is seeking love, you open yourself up to huge amounts of compassion for all with whom we share this beautiful earth. The frequency of love can be accessed by you, received by you, and given by you in any moment — to anyone around the world. You can send the energy of love out to all who need it and all who are hungry in their hearts. You will transform your experience of life when you learn to see through the ineffective methods people use to try and get love. Your heart expands for those who have closed themselves off from it, and you realize that all anyone ever wants is to love and be loved. Period. It all boils down to that.

For much of my life, I was not able to access love in the way that I know it now. Love was scary and I had a lot of fear around how much to reveal of my heart and who I could trust with it. Different people have different capacities to both love and be loved. It is tough for the ultra-sensitive to feel, because we often believe that other people can't meet us at the same depths we experience. This was the case for me most of my life and so I learned to temper my love and to hide it. I learned to be very protective over my heart and not to let it open too deeply or shine too brightly. I spent most of my life trying to feel safe, and in all of these often misguided attempts, I was trying to get back to the pure essence of me. As scared as I was to be fully present to the love inside of me, I also knew I wanted to live my life feeling fully and expressing openly.

Different people

have different capacities to both love and be loved.

Like any transformation, the old must become so constricting or annoying that the desire to change is worth the pain of breaking through. The moment just before the transformation occurs is often unbearable. Imagine a butterfly struggling to find its way out of the cocoon. It has to fight to break free from the too-tight container that was once its very cozy home. Feeling like it may be dying, not knowing what is happening or how this struggle will turn out. Finally, it emerges from the white mess, spreads its wings, experiences flight for the first time, and life is never again the same.

Just like that, the pain of living with a wall around my heart eventually became so great that I broke through it to a new experience of life and of love; but only after making my way through a very important, necessary human struggle. Releasing years of hoping, asking, and wanting to be seen by those who were never meant to see me, finally allowed me to love people freely—because I now needed nothing from them. But, you can't get to that place of accepting what *is*, without first experiencing the struggle of wanting and wishing people in your life to be different; of needing them to show up for you, listen better, and understand you more; repeatedly asking them to be more supportive or sensitive.

You have to almost be driven crazy by the futility of your own expectations before you surrender to the truth that certain people will never be at a level of consciousness that allows them to see your heart, and this is all okay. Each of us comes into this life with an agreement to grow our consciousness to a certain point, and it is all perfect. I am truly grateful for everyone who has crossed my path—those who poked at me, those who didn't get me, those who projected their stuff onto me, those who challenged me, those who pushed me further than I ever thought possible, and those who loved, supported, cared for, and uplifted me. It takes time to get to the love, and I certainly wasn't always there; but it comes in time.

Please know that if you are struggling to love someone else or yourself, that this is perfect. You can't bypass the internal struggle that is part and parcel in any process of transformation. This struggle is your rite of passage. Whether they are currently in your life or not is perfect. Trust yourself, trust your evolution, and trust your transformation, because every piece of it is leading you to a new frequency of love. The road is bumpy, messy, all-important, and worth every moment. Enjoy the ride and be happy that you chose the perfect people to trigger all the necessary insights within you in order to cultivate the one thing you need most: your own love.

Celebration

It's time to get this soul-infused, cosmic party started! Out with the champagne and rich food! In with some Dr. Dre, a little running man, and an intergalactic celebration in your honor for taking this deep dive into the blue waters of your own consciousness. Here's to raising the roof of infinite possibility in your own life! Celebration is a very high frequency energy. It is a beautiful way of showing gratitude for everything that's come into your life. You can celebrate through a party, by doing something nice for yourself, spending time in the company of high frequency friends, or even taking a day to be in nature. Whatever gets you excited, fills your heart, and honors your soul is powerful. Celebrating at every step along the journey affirms your gratitude for all that is manifesting around you, and expands even further what is possible. Your experience of life will shift at the precise rate that you're willing to celebrate everything, down to the minute details.

Celebration
is a very high frequency energy. It is a beautiful way of showing gratitude for everything that's come into your life.

Creating rituals of celebration brings us to a new level of being and raises the frequency of every aspect of your inner and outer life. Celebrate the lengths your inner truth has gone to in order to get your attention. Celebrate the limiting mindsets you've ditched, the outworn expectations you've released, the power you've found in your ability to create, the new experiences that are now available to you as a result, and the experience of discovering a tribe that feels like home so you can align and anchor in your soul frequency.

Inspired Action

- Reflect on each area of your life and see where you can bring celebration in as a ritual—within yourself, your family, friends, or your work environment.
- How could you bring the energy of celebration into the culture of your company or into the fabric of your home?
- Find positive, self-affirming ways to celebrate everything that is positive in your life.

From My Heart to Yours

I have such deep reverence for what it is to be human. I could not have made it through my own transformation without the people who showed up in my life to contribute, hold space for me, guide me to the next step, and show me the light when I felt lost. This is the beauty of alignment in our lives. We need others and they need us. This is how we make it in this world. Together.

Life is many things, and it takes great courage to see it through with your eyes open. I have won at some things and failed at others. I have cried on the floor in isolation and I have stood on stages receiving the powerful energy of love from countless others. I have been devastated and broken up with and I have been infused with love and joined in marriage. I have watched my son being born and held my grandmother's hand as she passed on. I have suffered disease and I have healed. I have been closed off and broken open many, many times over. I have sat quietly waiting and I have anxiously paced. I have seen things beyond the physical world and I have watched miracles take place right before my eyes. I am both human and more than human, and so are you. And I am deeply grateful for you, for your willingness to see beyond the mundane to the extraordinary. To take the road less traveled and to be the stand for a new way of living life; one rooted in LOVE + TRUTH where miracles are a way of life, where your gifts are illuminated, and your value is celebrated by all who cross your path.

So, here we are. We've reached the end only to discover, of course, that it is just the beginning. You have everything it takes to be all of YOU. And guess what, when you are all of YOU—bold in your truth, released from the past, fully self-expressed in your experiences, and aligned with your highest self, it's interesting how addictions and struggles with food just fall away and how your life grows in the most beautiful and magical ways. It is never the diseases of body or mind, money, the lack of a relationship, or anything else that warrants your precious time and attention. Those are and have only ever been the smoke and mirrors keeping you looking in the wrong direction. When you free up your focus, a new energy begins to course through your veins. The all-expansive, rock star, off the charts consciousness that is the real you has been waiting on the sidelines so patiently for this next chapter, for your deeper awakening, and the dawning of your soul's powerful reign. It is high time to accept your crown as the queen of manifestation and mastery, and allow your soul frequency to freely beam its radiance all over your life and the lives of everyone you encounter. This is your purpose.

The journey is deep and vast, extraordinary and fulfilling, and something not to be missed. There is no one in your way, and there never has been. Not your parents, your spouse, siblings, bosses, friends, or society. You hold the key to freeing yourself and you're the only one who can do it. Become the rebel. Create YOUR way through this profound transformation and shine your light on this world. When you step forward, we all do.

And always remember, I see you. I support you. You've got this. Now, go out there and live like you mean it.

Inspired Action
Reflections on Align

There are so many ways to start tuning your ear to the whispers of your soul, and one of the most immediate ways to access this frequency is through a regular practice of meditation, mindfulness, or resting in silence.

There is no right way to do this, but the practice of BEING is important to hearing the soul frequency. If closed-eye meditation seems too intimidating, you can dive into the same silence by focusing your attention on the flame of a candle, or put on some peaceful music and sit quietly. This is how we tune into the call and discover what is next for us. We live in a world where busy is praised, as if somehow you are better or of greater value if you are busy. And yet all of that doingness keeps you disconnected from the whisper. You can't hear a whisper when your life is a rock concert.

And so, you will have to find a way to unwind and reconnect. You can begin by turning off your phone, looking someone in the eye, and exchanging energy intentionally by giving and receiving it in conversation. Another place to start is by frequency hacking your life. Releasing what no longer resonates is an important part of honoring your truth. A list of ways to frequency hack your life can be found in the Introspection section at the back of the book.

Introspection

Truth

Finding your truth requires questioning and introspection, calling on your deepest inner self to rise to the surface and be given a voice in your life. Here are some additional questions to contemplate your inner voice and true desires.

- What might happen if I don't listen to the calling?
- What happens if I hold onto something no longer meant for me?
- What might be possible in my life if I stepped forward in faith?
- What is my soul seeking to express in this lifetime?
- What parts of myself have I shut down?
- What dreams, interests, and desires have I given up on?
- What am I afraid to admit to myself?
- If I were to express my most courageous self, how would that look? What would I think, speak, or do differently?
- What discomfort or pain do I feel in my body?
- What, if any, diagnosable illnesses do I have? What was going on in my life at their onset?

Introspection

- What parts of my body do I feel are not working optimally?
- What do I turn to when I'm stressed or angry?
- What are my "go to" foods, beverages, and behaviors when life doesn't go my way?
- What strategies do I use to "keep the lid" on my emotions?
- What changes do I know I need to make to become healthier—physically, mentally, emotionally, and spiritually?

Release

If you knew that anything your heart desires is possible, and you had the tools to create it, what would you create? Here are some questions to get you thinking:

- Do you want to work? If so, what type of work lights you up inside?
- Do you have a family? What does a great family life look like?
- Do you have a life partner? Many partners? Or does being single sound more exciting?
- Where do you want to live?
- Do you want to travel? How often? Where to?
- What does your financial life look like?
- Do you have tons of friends? Just a special few? Or a bunch of acquaintances?
- What makes you feel empowered?
- What is your daily routine? Or is every day different?
- Is your health important? If so, what do you do to maintain it?
- Are you an animal lover?

- Do you like to take big risks or play it safe?
- Do you give time, money or assistance to charities?
- What is your biggest dream? And what would it be like to live it?

Experience

Begin to play around with the art of deliberately shifting the direction of your thoughts.

Make the decision to go cold turkey on gossip, complaining, and any other conversations that bring you down.

When you catch yourself in the middle of a negative thought pattern, consciously do something to shift it.

A great way to do this is by moving your body physically: get up, walk around, and if time permits, go outside! Maintaining a sedentary posture for too long makes the body restless and cranky, and soon our thoughts mirror this discontent. Movement will get your blood pumping, while also giving you a fresh perspective on whatever subject you were previously having negative thoughts about.

Strive to become a master at thought shifting by making a commitment to practice, practice, practice. Negative thoughts, feelings, and moods are always going to surface; but that doesn't mean you need to greet each one with a warm beverage and a welcome mat. In fact, you don't need to indulge them for more than a few seconds—and the sooner you can redirect your attention, the more powerful a creator you will become.

So for example, when a worrisome thought about someone you love pops into your mind, acknowledge that you have the power to nourish that thought until it blossoms into a full-blown tree in the garden of your mind, or to stop it right at the trunk before any momentum gets rolling.

Conserve your mental energy so that it can be used to create experiences that you love, rather than those you dislike or merely tolerate.

Finally, when you're getting yourself ready in the morning, take some time to notice and appreciate the things about yourself that you genuinely love. To make this even more powerful, speak these things out loud to yourself in the mirror.

At first glance, these practices might seem trivial, but the power of these actions builds over time. Like a pianist practicing scales or a child who is learning how to pedal a bike with the support of training wheels, all efforts you make in shifting your mindset to the positive are strengthening your mental discipline and carving new neuropathways in your brain. If practiced often enough, a new road that leads to love of self and others will become your automatic go-to route.

Align

Make a list of the top ten people in your life—the people who you spend the most time around or the most time talking to on the phone. Then, in order to get a sense of the dominant energetic frequency of each relationship, answer the following questions with either a 'yes' or 'no' for each of these people:

- Is this person living their purpose in the world?
- Has this person done work on himself or herself in order to better understand their life and their motivations?
- Does this person bring more joy or drama into your life?
- Does this person lift you up or tear you down?
- Does this person believe in the vision you hold for your life?
- Is being in alignment with this person helping you to live your purpose?

It may seem difficult or strange to evaluate your relationships in this way, and you may think, 'What does it really matter if my future vision is supported?' or 'We've been friends for years,' or 'This person is family.' I certainly understand all of these sentiments, and I've considered all of these things myself in taking an honest look at the way I spend my time and the people who I surround myself with. The truth is that you cannot have what you want without giving up the people holding you back from it, and beginning to connect with those who are going to support it.

Acknowledgements

Acknowledgements

I am going to cry writing this because this has been such a journey. It all started over two years ago, when I was getting an intuitive reading and the person told me that I was going to write a book in the next six months. I thought she was crazy! I was the Mom of a small child, a wife, and building a business with long hours and a whole lot of passion and energy being infused into it. There was no burning idea brewing under the surface. I had nothing that I knew of that needed to be shared. I was at a loss and chalked this up to a fluke.

It wasn't but a few weeks later that I ran into another friend who said he thought I would write book. Then a weekend later I attended a conference and one of the speakers kept repetitively saying, *write the book, write the book, write the book.* By this point I felt like I was being singled out and the speaker was talking directly to me. I felt like the whole room was looking at me and I remember thinking—*okay,*

okay, I got it! But, what's it supposed to be about? Can you help a sister out?

Still overwhelmed, my dear friend and coach, Gary Quinn, who had always told me that there was a book in me, told me to create an outline. I sat at the computer and my fingers started moving and before I knew it, I had page after page of a very rough outline. It seemed as though it came from somewhere else. Words cannot do justice to what Gary has meant to my life. He has been a friend, a brother and a supporter even during the moments I have been falling apart and needed someone to lift me up. You, Gary, are an earth angel. A champion for good and I am eternally grateful for you and all that you have brought into my life in big and small ways. I love you!

After we had an outline, Gary connected me with Danielle Dorman, the best writer, editor, and word fairy ever. From the time we met, it was like magic, yo! Danielle shares my love for old school rap, her middle name is LEE, and she has loved this project and guided me to my best self with every word. Girl, you are a cosmic boomerang in my life. Don't know what I did to deserve the kind of fun we have had, but I am so fortunate—it's almost stupid. Thanks for all of the word play, fun, collaboration, and for riding this wave with me. I am so blessed to have crossed your path and there is so much more to come—now that the flood-gates are open, it's on, for shizzle!

Once the book was almost complete, Paulina Jaeger-Rosete stepped in to work her magic and clean up all of my typos and improper use of grammar. She also, pushed me to think, go deeper in some parts, and made sure I was making sense. I am a girl with massive downloads, but they certainly don't come in perfect English. So, Paulina—thank you for putting the finishing touches on this baby!

This book is my life, my heart and as you can imagine when you are about to share your life story through the lens of your own powerful transformation, it almost takes your breath away. The creative process always pulls up fear to be released as you step forward into the unknown. This book almost took my breath away too many times to count!

To Dad—I can't tell you how much it makes me cry to thank my Dad for bringing me into this life, for being patient with all of the ways I am so uniquely unique, and for supporting me in ways that are extraordinary while I figured out how to express myself in the world. You have saved me many times. You are an incredible force of nature, human being and I am blessed to be your daughter. Thank you for always teaching me that I could do anything I put my mind to. I truly know that now, with every fiber of my being. I love you!

To Mom—Thank you for giving me life, one of the most important gifts a person can give. You have taught me the most incredible lessons in life, even when you didn't realize you were teaching them, lessons that have been monumentally important for me. I am so grateful for the journey and the lessons and I love you!

To my family in heaven who I know had a hand in writing this book. There are so many of you and while it can feel like a relationship ends when one leaves human form, boy, is that not true. My relationships with you have deepened and taken on new form.

Grandma Dorothy—you are my light—my @pinklite to be exact. I love you more today than yesterday and I miss your warm loving hugs—watching Donohue with you and Grandpa after school with a snack. You and Grandpa were all love, and the coolest grandparents ever. The safe and warm space you provided me as a child was everything to me. Thank you for seeing me. I love you both!

Billy Pinecone, my Dad #2, words cannot express the ways you have touched my heart and my life. You are the most fun, funny, and kind person, not to mention the smartest person that I knew and know. You must be rocking the heavens up there! It was an honor to be with you at the end of your life and it is beyond incredible that you have stayed with me ever since. Creating new opportunities, sharing secrets, and guiding me in the cleverest ways. You are such a solid soul who has such integrity—I honor you with all that I am and I love you! P.S. thanks for all of the feathers!

To my sisters, Tracy and Michal Sue: Life brings people together in the most mysterious ways and yet, God knew we were meant to be sisters. Both of you have hearts of gold and I am so honored to call you sisters. Tracy, I can't even believe your strength and your journey. You make me so happy and proud and you have so many wonderful blessings to share with others. Michal Sue, you remind me of your Dad, just pure goodness all the way through.

Acknowledgements

Thank you for your love and support and here's to living free forever! And I love the brothers too! Not leaving you guys out, thanks for being the kind and generous men that you are. I love you!

To my circle of sister goddesses who have held me when I cried, helped me to grow and be courageous, and made me feel beautiful and loved even when I had mascara pouring down my face. You are the embodiment of the divine feminine and I can't believe I have the honor of knowing you. Mary McPherson, you are an angel in my life and have provided such safety and comfort during times of great change. You are a powerful healer and an ancient soul. Jessilynn Gilbank, you have believed in me and been a champion in my life in more way that I can count. You are the embodiment of Shamanism and I love every conversation, dance, connection, and collaboration. Heather Premac, you are a body whisperer and a soulful advocate for all women to have freedom from the past and be free of the ties that bind. You are a light for this world and a goddess in every way showing people how to live from their hearts. Jules Ball, I want to live and die in your beautiful clothes. I have never felt so beautiful and in alignment than when I have your designs on me. You all mean the world to me, I couldn't have made it through without you and I love you!

To every single teacher who has crossed my path, the ones that opened me up, connected me, pushed me, broke me down and built me up, I am grateful. From the red rocks of Sedona with Bahkta, to the most incredible circle of women curated by Grace Cavanaugh and Osirah, to Star Magic with Jerry Sargeant, to the journeying with Trevor Green. These moments and experiences live in my heart and mind forever. In little and big ways you have all contributed to my journey and may not even realize the profound significance you have made in my life. Thank you all for your love and for speaking your truth so that I could find mine. I love you!

To my lifelong circle of sisters, Andrea Andes, Erica Haupert, Allison August, Lauren Pittman, Kira Heuer who have grown up with me and were the source of so much fun its ridiculous. I can't even believe some of the things we did and lived to tell. I am so grateful for the laughs, the fun, the trips, the experiences, the memories and the growth over so many years. Thank you for loving me and being there for me. I love you!

Amber Susa Jewett (Susanator)! We have had quite the journey since childhood and it is beyond words how full circle our paths have been. I am so freaking proud of you and excited for you! You are a powerful creator of amazing things and this is only the beginning of what is to come. I can't wait to watch all that is expanding in your life. You are a bright shiny soul, one heck of a powerful woman. Thank you for walking with path with me, I love you!

To my amazing clients, you are my "why." What you may not know is how much I cry when things are tough for you and how much I celebrate when you win. It is personal for me and you are incredible human beings who are living life to the fullest. I love courageous people and you define that fully. It is awesome and I am in awe daily. Thank you for sharing your stories, your hearts and allowing me to be a part of your lives. I am honored and it is everything! I love you!

To Kamilah Marshall, you are a powerful beacon of light, you beautiful human, you! I have watched you spread your wings in ways that give me goose bumps—cheek goose bumps! There is only greatness ahead on your path and I can't wait to watch it unfold more and more each day. Thank you for being YOU, my friend. I love you!

To Shoshana Bean, to watch you give big is something every human should get to experience. You are a powerful force and a beautiful soul wrapped up in one. Your ability to push the limits of your creativity is everything. I could not be more excited for what you are creating! AND thank you for your lending your magic to The Soul Frequency mission. YOU rock, my friend! I love you!

To Eden Espinosa, your beautiful fairy energy is a gift to this world. Watching you do YOU makes me so freaking happy. There is nothing you can't do when standing in your power. The work you are creating and will continue to create in truth will be nothing short of magical! Watching it all is so beautiful, my friend! I love you!

To my amazing colleagues and friends who are transforming health and consciousness on this planet, you are incredible warriors courageous and passionate and it is an honor to call you friends. Thank you to Dr. Deanna, Teri, Debora, Amy, Wendy, Niki, Dr. Keesha, Bloom, Christine, David, Katie, Sarina, Laura, Jay, Dr. Carol, Rachel, Brodie, Melissa,

Matt, Brian, Ani, Caspar, Dr. Kim, Clarissa, Anne, Dr. Joy, Megan, Ryan, Teddy, Erin, Dr. Michelle, Nicolas, Autumn, Chas, Dr. Fine, Meg, Kristen, Diane, Dr. Jolene, Dr. Maya, Julie, Cynthia, Leslie, Ann, Tricia, Andrea, Amanda, Belinda, Christine, and Johnny for the work you do and for sharing your hearts and minds for the betterment of others. It is a big mission and I love you for taking it on.

To Dr. Eric Z and Mama Z, you two are miracle workers together and I am so happy our paths crossed. You are amazing friends and ancient, loving souls. Thank you Eric, for all of your guidance and support and for all that you have openly shared with me that has made my life and business better. Sabrina, you are a powerhouse of a woman and you will continue to share your light in some incredible ways and I can't wait to be witness to it. Love you guys!

To The Soul Frequency Team—Jendi, Sarah, Kyla and Collin—and supporters along the way, none of this would be possible without you. Seriously, this is a collective and you are the inspiration and drive that makes everything run. I am so honored that you feel inspired by this mission and want to share your time with me creating things to empower and uplift humanity. I am grateful for you, your brilliance and the knowledge that you share that makes our digital home—TheSoulFrequency.com— a place that is welcoming and loving. I love you all!

Oh boy, cue the tears, where do I begin. I can't even write. To MY Love, Travis, you are everything I always hoped you would be and more. You are beyond who I thought